Your Wildest Dreams, Wi... loud, and at the same ti... *language?* you'll find yo... else will you read the ph... find the word "robot" alongside "with a bartending degree." This is to say that Mike Sacks is not just a sensational comic writer, but a sensational writer—period.

—DAVID SEDARIS

Any book that has funny jokes about porno, robots, and Shaft has to be good. And this one is.

—JACK HANDEY

This humor collection is packed with winners. In one of my many favorites, "The Rejection of Anne Frank," a publisher slams the fifteen-year-old girl's diary for trailing off at the end. What more do you want, America? Mike Sacks is hilarious, unique, and possibly crazy. You should definitely buy his book, or at the very least, steal it from somewhere.

—SIMON RICH, writer for *Saturday Night Live*;
author of *Ant Farm: And Other Desperate Situations*,
Free-Range Chickens, and *Elliot Allagash*

This book is super funny but also very human, which is my favorite kind of comedy. Mike Sacks is a very smart and talented guy. Now if he'd just pay me back that money he owes me.

—PAUL FEIG, creator of *Freaks and Geeks*;
author of *Kick Me: Adventures in Adolescence*
and *Superstud: Or How I Became a 24-Year-Old Virgin*

"A blurb," as Mike Sacks explains in his book, is "a glowing remark on the back cover written by an author or TV chef." Here's my glowing remark: This is a very, very funny book.

—A. J. JACOBS, contributing writer, *Esquire*; author of
The Guinea Pig Diaries and *The Year of Living Biblically*

Sacks has an uncanny ability to see through the BS of modern life and into what really makes us tick. Which would be depressing as hell, if it weren't so funny.

—SAM MEANS, writer for *The Daily Show* and author of *A Practical Guide to Racism*

In the world of humor writing, a Mike Sacks story is a must read. Sacks's short pieces walk the fine line between clever and ridiculous. Not quite high-brow or low-brow, but more upper-middle-brow. They shop at Whole Foods, but still go to Dunkin' Donuts. In short, his stories make us want to buy inordinately priced organic produce and fried dough. If this does not make him a national treasure, then we must redefine the meaning of the term.

—CHRISTOPHER MONKS, editor, *McSweeneys.net*

Mike Sacks rehabilitated me from a deep, dark depression. I nursed from his teat, followed his gentle wisdom, and now I'm doing much better. Book's great, too.

—ERIC WAREHEIM, *Tim and Eric Awesome Show*

Though many people continue to believe that Mike Sacks is little more than a nonexistent cryptid, like Bigfoot or the Loch Ness Monster, this book proves once and for all that he is real. And that he is brilliant. And if you walk around with this book in your hands, people will think you're brilliant!

—JASON EATON, author of *The Facttracker*

The funniest book since Woody Allen's *Getting Even*, without nearly as many references to the Talmud.

—DANA BROWN, senior articles editor, *Vanity Fair*

In *Your Wildest Dreams*, Mike Sacks claims one of the worst places to die is "on a toilet . . . reading this book," but I would be proud to have anyone discover my body clutching this hilarious volume, as long as I had flushed first.

—MIKE SWEENEY, head writer for *Late Night with Conan O'Brien*, *Tonight Show with Conan O'Brien*, *Conan*

Your Wildest Dreams, Within Reason is an eclectic treasure of humor, and the ludicrous suggestion that a pretty blonde would work at Gray's Papaya.

—BRIAN SACK, author of *In the Event of My Untimely Demise*

Laughter can be found on nearly every page of this collection. Except, of course, for page eighty-seven. There is nothing on that page but unflagging horror and despair.

—DAN GUTERMAN, head writer, *The Onion*

Mike Sacks takes on the narration personae of the hapless, the moronic, the pathetic, and the administratively inclined in order to save comedic prose, yes, but more importantly to make you laugh in that twitchy, awkward way that is hugely sincere, but also unbecoming on the subway.

—JULIE KLAUSNER, writer for *Best Week Ever with Paul F. Tompkins* and Robert Smigel's *TV Funhouse*; author of *I Don't Care About Your Band*

Sacks's wit isn't just razor sharp—it's as sharp as the tool that a mohel brings to a circumcision. And it's just as likely to leave its beneficiary gasping for air . . . and, for some reason, lox.

—ROB KUTNER, writer for *The Daily Show*, *Tonight Show with Conan O'Brien*; author of *Apocalypse How: Turn the End-Times into the Best of Times!*

With *Your Wildest Dreams*, Mike Sacks proves himself to be one of today's best humor writers. He also proves himself to be completely and utterly out of his mind. Seriously, I don't want this guy anywhere near me or any of my stuff.

—JON WURSTER, *The Best Show on WFMU*

Like most comedy savants, Mike Sacks knows too much about the human condition to interact with us. Seriously, if fate puts you anywhere near this guy, steer clear. Read this book instead. It's sharp, knowing, and laugh-out-loud funny—and, unlike Mike, not hazardous to your health.

—FRANK DIGIACOMO, the only person in
The Aristocrats who didn't get a single laugh

I would call Mike Sacks's *Your Wildest Dreams, Within Reason* a fantastic bathroom read, but no one should ever laugh that hard in a bathroom. That would be like something out of a Mike Sacks piece. A great, great collection.

—CHRIS REGAN, co-author of *America (The Book)*;
author of *Mass Historia: 365 Days of Historical
Facts and (Mostly) Fictions*

Why surf the Web for hours trying (unsuccessfully) to find something funny, when you can just pick up this book and surf Mike Sacks's brilliant brain? Funny tweets, texts, stories, lists, confessions, rules, and even dirty pictures—all between these two covers, and with no cookies or pop-ups.

—DAVID MINER, producer, manager, and
partner at 3 Arts Entertainment

Your Wildest Dreams,
Within Reason

Your Wildest Dreams, Within Reason

Mike Sacks

Tin House Books
Portland, Oregon & New York, New York

Copyright © 2011 Mike Sacks

Illustrations © 2011 Tae Won Yu

Additional copyright information on pages 268–269

Published by Tin House Books, Portland, Oregon, and New York, New York

Distributed to the trade by Publishers Group West, 1700 Fourth St., Berkeley, CA 94710, www.pgw.com

Library of Congress Cataloging-in-Publication Data

Sacks, Mike.

Your wildest dreams, within reason / by Mike Sacks ; illustrations by Tae Won Yu. — 1st U.S. ed.

    p. cm.

ISBN 978-1-935639-02-2

1. American wit and humor. I. Title.

PN6165.S24 2011

814'.6—dc22

                              2010032807

First U.S. edition 2011

Printed in Canada

Interior design: Jim Hill and Diane Chonette

www.tinhouse.com

For Kate and Little D.

"In my wildest imagination, as limited as one such exists, I never did once consider I'd end up in such an odd, curious situation. This begets that, and it's time to die. Please tell my wife to water the flower-bed."

**—Last words of Jaele Wheeler,
accused murderer of the "Seneca Seven,"
Poolesville, Maryland, 1914**

ATTENTION READERS:

This Is a Warning!

The pieces contained within this book were first published in *The New Yorker*, *Vanity Fair*, *McSweeney's*, *Esquire*, *Vice*, and any number of other publications, including a few which no longer exist.

But that's not what I'm warning you about. Here's what I'm warning you about: The vast majority of these short humor pieces—or the random list, the occasional illustration, other effluvia—have absolutely *nothing* to do with each other. There is no overarching theme, no recurring characters, nothing that links one piece to another. There are exceptions, but this is mainly the case.

I'm hoping that if you don't like this book, it has nothing to do with that fact. (It will be for any number of reasons, but probably not that one.)

With that off my chest, and it's been sitting there patiently for the last six years, I'd like to say one more thing: I have many terrifically talented writer friends, and I'm lucky enough to have had the opportunity to work with them these past few years. Collectively, they are known as the Pleasure Syndicate. Individually, they are Todd Levin, Scott Jacobson, Jason Roeder, and Ted Travelstead. In addition, I have worked with Bob Powers, Scott Rothman, Will Tracy, and Teddy Wayne. I make special mention in the table of contents when a piece was co-written with one or more of these fine writers. Seek out their work.

Okay, that's it. See you at Pop's . . .

Table of Contents

Whoops!

To: All Staff
9:12 AM
Subject: Whoops, Sorry About that Last E-Mail!

I'd just like to apologize for the last e-mail, which I
sent to "All Staff." I meant to send it to my friend Alex
Stafford. It was a mistake. Sorry.

To: All Staff
10:14 AM
Subject: Clarification on Apology E-Mail!

I want to apologize for not being entirely clear in my
last e-mail. Let me try to be more specific: originally, I

was attempting to send my friend Alex Stafford (not All Staff) an e-mail on horses and how I've always liked to watch horses run. I then made a leap into the realm of the imaginary. Again, I do apologize.

To: All Staff
11:01 AM
Subject: re: what the fuck?!

Wow. Today just ain't my day! I've been told that I have more "explaining" to do, re: "the realm of the imaginary." So here goes: I probably should have told you that for the past two years, give or take a few months, I've imagined myself as a talking horse and that, as this talking horse, I've ruled a fantasy kingdom populated by you guys, my co-workers. The 27 images I included in the first e-mail are, in fact, Photoshop montages, not actual photos. Carry on!

To: All Staff
12:20 PM
Subject: re: You Have More Explaining to Do About Those Images!

There are days and there are *days*! Perhaps I'm not expressing myself as well as I should. I guess that's why I'm in accounting and not PR! Okay, let's start from the very beginning. In this imaginary world I've created, I'm a talking horse. Simple. You guys are my servants. All of you have kept your real names, but your "imaginary" selves have taken on new roles in my fantasy land. A quick example:

"Mary Jenkins" from benefits is a fair maiden who was born in a tiny stable and grew up to fall in love with

"Chris Topp" from payroll, who works as a candle maker and sleeps behind the bar in the tavern run by "Wayne Harris" from the mailroom, who is secretly seeing "April Kelly" from office services, who works as my "horse girl" and soaps me down every night before I sleep on my bed of hay. Is this making more sense? For the record, all the Photoshop images are a combination of photos found on the Internet and your headshots from the company directory. Steve, I'm about ready for lunch if you are.

To: All Staff
1:23 PM
Subject: re: I Feel Violated!!!

Imagine my surprise to return from lunch only to find hundreds of e-mails in the ol' inbox! Seems that quite a few of you have additional questions concerning the roles that each of you play within my magical fantasy land. Sigh. It's really quite simple:

"Hope Marks" from the nurse's office refuses to sleep with "Darryl Russell" from security because Darryl is a centaur (see image #6) and Hope is a unicorn (image #3). "Kathryn Haynes" from marketing has caught wind of this because she was born with oversize ears (image #14) and can hear literally everything. She also tends to walk around the village nude (image #8) and sleep with anyone who happens to be available; in one instance, she cavorts with "Jamie Devine" from payroll by the banks of a river, as "Betsy Schneider" and "Krista Stark" from the cafeteria look on in wonder (image #7). I also look on in wonder (images #4 and #5).

In another instance, "Katy Devine" from special projects climbs to the top of the bell tower that's located on my castle and makes love to "Doug Benson" from security, as "Jessica McNally" from the nurse's office braids my tail in a most tender fashion (image #11). She is not wearing a top (image #12) or a bottom (image #13).

Meanwhile, "Alexis Weber" from the front office is an angry dwarf in need of gold. He has just taken on an assignment to kill "Bob Simmons" from purchasing, but only after he has promised "Marina DelGado" from human resources that he will turn her into a good witch by way of a magical spell. This magical spell consists of having sex with a complete stranger ("Mitch Fitzgerald," also from human resources) while riding a white mare, ass-back and fancy free, across a great plain (image #9). The horse, if you haven't already guessed, is me (image #1). In the background, if you look closely enough, you can just make out "Joe Griggs" from janitorial looking on in wonder (image #2).

Whew! Done! By the way, anyone have the forms for the Milner project? I really need them by this afternoon. Thanks!

To: All Staff
3:12 PM
Subject: re: you're sick!

Holy cripes! Sometimes I wonder if anyone besides me gets any work done around here! I step away from my desk for two seconds and I come back to discover that a thousand more questions have been posed! Don't get me wrong: I think it's super that all of you are taking an active interest in my fantasy kingdom, but my goodness! So let me just tie up one loose end and let me do it real, real quick, because I've just been notified that I've been fired:

Yes, that is you, "Samantha Rymer" from expenses, standing next to a razzleberry bush in image #15. And yes, Samantha, that is indeed a crown of doves perched atop your head, and no, Samantha, those are not your real breasts (images #16-27).

Everyone up to date? I'm really gonna miss all of you! I feel we've become especially close over these past two years! And that even goes for "Marina the Good Witch" from human resources! I honestly did not know that "good witches" could get so angry! LOL!

Your Imaginary Leader Who's Now Waving Goodbye, As Kathy from Security Hangs on Tightly and Rides Him (see attached image),

MIKE THE TALKING HORSE

A Leaflet Dropped over Amy Weller's House

Amy Weller, my girlfriend, my love, please look up. The thousands of brightly colored leaflets that you see cascading down from this rented airplane can only mean one thing: I am an extremely successful businessman, community leader, boyfriend, bon vivant. There is no denying these facts.

To think otherwise would be 100 percent wrong.

MORE FACTS:

Mike Sacks is **dynamite**, strong, captivating. Mike Sacks enjoys reading to senior citizens. Mike Sacks enjoys cooking **delicious** hot meals for strangers. Mike Sacks enjoys telling funny stories, **softly** and **clearly**, to immigrants and to children and, on occasion, to the infirm. You didn't know about all of this? It's <u>**true**</u>!

WOW!

There is just so much that Amy Weller does not know about her boyfriend, Mike Sacks, whom she has not seen for two weeks and who now goes by the slightly more exciting, **grown-up**, and **respectable** name of MICHAEL SACKS.

But what's that you're thinking? MICHAEL SACKS is an out-of-work furniture salesman, and has been ever since he slipped on that spilled Frappuccino outside a Starbucks in the Congressional Strip Mall, Rockville, Maryland (June 24th)?

And what's that you're also thinking? Could this MICHAEL SACKS be the same handsome-ish gentleman who for years pretended to search for a new job each morning only to end up sitting in a public library all day, sleeping off the effects of deep, unrelenting depression? Hey, not so fast!

Check out the photorealistic drawings of MICHAEL SACKS that are now being dropped via mini-parachutes into your hands! This new MICHAEL SACKS looks familiar, and yet just the slightest bit . . . **different**. Check out those **MUSCLES!**

But where did his handlebar mustache go? (Perhaps it no longer exists because MICHAEL SACKS at last came to realize that the mustache, although funny for ironic purposes, did occasionally smell like his last meal?)

You're confused. Could all this be for real?!

Why not? MICHAEL SACKS was terrific before, but now he's **superb**!

Do you need additional confirmation of these and other **facts**?

Turn on your computer at your earliest convenience and check out the **new** and **marvelous** website specializing in all things MICHAEL SACKS:

www.michaelsacks-michaelsacks.com
(Please note: www.michaelsacks.com was taken.)

There you will find a preview of what can be expected from the New & Improved MICHAEL SACKS in the exciting year ahead:

The porch, formerly attached to
Amy Weller's house, to be rebuilt after last summer's
errant firecracker explosion!

•

A fund-raising cookie sale to
pay off the debt owed to the
Jet Ski dealership!

•

Cosmetic surgery to remove that
tattoo of a third eye!

•

Surgery to remove that tattoo of a fourth eye!

•

A full and detailed explanation for the illegal backyard petting zoo, the one that Amy Weller did not learn about until the authorities were notified by neighbors "concerned" about "manure" in the "water supply"

**(Additional Exciting Projects
TBA, September 14,
at a press conference,
T.G.I. Friday's, Route 355!!!)**

Hey, Amy Weller, didja know???!!!

- That MICHAEL SACKS has at last, and of his own accord, thrown out his entire collection of T-shirts with funny sayings (including his favorite: "Born to Pump!"), even though he's owned them all for years and they're still incredibly **comfy**? You see, it's time to MOVE ON and GROW UP.

- That MICHAEL SACKS has a newfound respect for Amy Weller's need for **peace** and **quiet**, and will support her in this desire by not practicing the knee-cymbals at all hours of the day and night, even though he's dreamed of learning how to play them since watching Dick Van Dyke in *Mary Poppins*? It's time to be a little less SELFISH and a little more RESPECTFUL of other people's FEELINGS.

- That MICHAEL SACKS no longer has time for friends with **rhyming nicknames** and **bad habits**, including the buddy who is prone to spitting indoors and urinating out? It's time to hang with a NEW CROWD, and to earn a living, perhaps by toiling away for LONG HOURS and MINIMUM WAGE at the small lawn-care business that Amy Weller's father owns.

Amy Weller, what is in a name exactly? If that name is **MICHAEL SACKS**, tons!

MICHAEL SACKS = A man who looks forward to moving back into Amy Weller's house and acting **responsibly**, this time by contributing to the mortgage with authentic currency and not with scraps of paper with "Will Pay Later" written on them in crayon.

MICHAEL SACKS = A man with **goals** and **ambition**, a boyfriend whom Amy Weller can be proud to bring to public gatherings, who will no longer embarrass Amy Weller at said events by getting drunk and performing his imitation of two wild monkeys coupling.

Yo, girl! There is so much to look **forward** to with the New & Improved MICHAEL SACKS!

Are U Ready 2 Take a Chance on Something Wonderful?

Amy Weller, if the answer is **YES**, please understand that your life's savings of $13,000 that was **borrowed** for this campaign was well worth it!!! Look way up in the sky! See that man waving from the airplane? He has so much to offer you! Stick out your arms and be prepared to scoop up the **MICHAEL SACKS** hats, **MICHAEL SACKS** T-shirts, **MICHAEL SACKS** beer cozies, and **MICHAEL SACKS** bumper stickers, all yours to keep . . . for ABSOLUTELY FREE!!! Are you convinced now? How about if **MICHAEL SACKS** unfurls the following banner?

MICHAEL SACKS:
Successful Boyfriend, Community Leader, <u>Businessman!</u>

Convinced now? BEAUTIFUL!!!

Sweetheart . . . if there is any possible way that the
New & Improved MICHAEL SACKS can figure out how to
land this rented plane, he shall be home shortly, moving
van in tow. Please have dinner waiting?

—**MICHAEL SACKS,**

Certified Private Pilot (April, projected)
Please see reverse side for exciting details!

Saw You on the Q Train

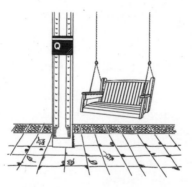

Saw you on the Q train, late afternoon, March 7. You were wearing a red dress, carrying a black purse. Departed at Broadway. Too shy to say hi. Respond here?

Never done this before. Am responding! Now what? **Black Purse**.

New for me as well. Tell me about yourself. **Q Train**.

Interests: Movies, jogging, gardening. Yours? **Purse**.

I, too, enjoy gardening: Have always dreamed of owning a country home, perhaps far, far away. To awaken each morning to the trilling of canaries. **Q**.

Dreaming of that perfect home, that flawless slice of land. Ah, yes, to live amidst nature! To create, from out of the ashes of nothingness, a dream fashioned into reality. A bed of flowers in the springtime. Newly sprung vegetables. A rebirth of sorts. I love it! **Purse**.

This house of which we speak. Ivory-colored clapboard with blue trim? A red picket fence? A crushed-gravel path winding toward a mahogany-topped gazebo? Within it we shall sit, eating the fruits of our gardening labors. **Q**.

I picture a house more beautiful than those found in the fanciest of periodicals. Rosebushes next to a babbling brook. A handcrafted swing. A couple in love rocking into days and nights of firefly-lit wonder. Two children, perhaps with the names Audrey and Jonah. The perfect home, a perfect life. **Purse**.

Yes, two beautiful kids, two ideal names! A babbling brook, there is nothing more luxurious! But the swing, so silly. **Q**.

Children with doe-like eyes, so wise for their years, I can see them now! And there is nothing more luxurious than a babbling brook! But no swing? **Purse**.

Something so gauche about a swing, no? Too Maurice Chevalier. Not enough Clark Gable. **Q**.

Clark Gable, indeed! One of my favorites. But, really, no swing? As a child growing up in the city, there was nothing that I wished for more . . . besides that perfect man! **Purse**.

Just something . . . how do I put this? A little too yearning, a tad too needy? Perhaps I'm not expressing myself well. **Q**.

A small swing, then? In the corner of a long porch? Overlooking the garden? While we enjoy freshly squeezed lemonade? From the lemon tree out back, just next to the badminton net? Perfection! **Purse**.

I'm just really . . . the garden, yes, the lemonade, I love it, badminton, fantastic. But the swing, honestly, I cannot approve. It's just—are you familiar with that life-insurance commercial, the one with the older gentleman and the elderly woman, they're swinging and they're talking? About death? Perhaps it's that connotation, perhaps something else, but it's not doing anything for me. I am so sorry. **Q**.

For me, I hate to say this, but the swing is the cherry on top, the dot beneath the exclamation point. The swing is everything! Without it, the house becomes a carcass, sans soul, sans meaning. Can you not compromise on this? A swing, as simple as it stands? Think about it? *Please*. **Purse**.

My love, I have thought long and hard about it, and as much as it pains me to write, I cannot accept the notion of a swing. I, too, have dreams. Dreams that include no reference to a swing. And for that I most sincerely apologize. **Q**.

You bastard. For this you extinguish our dreams, our desires? A goddamned swing? **Purse**.

I shall go one step further. A babbling brook? Gone. Your taste is suspect, that I knew from the start. **Q**.

And this coming from someone who wishes for a hideous red picket fence? The irony, it's delicious. **Purse**.

My darling, please. The swing we can talk about another time. We have our whole lives . . . **Q**.

But, really, a red picket fence? Is it your wish to construct a New Orleans-style bordello? **Purse**.

A bordello? I grew up with a red picket fence! Are you implying that I grew up in a whorehouse? **Q**.

I am implying nothing. Beyond the fact that I am unhappy. Perhaps it is not the swing. Perhaps it is more. **Purse**.

A separation? Is that what you're reaching for? Keep your dream house, the colors were all slightly off, the imaginary mortgage was beyond my grasp. Build your swing. Create your new life. **Q**.

That seems fair. But can we not work it out? Could it possibly be too late? **Purse**.

The children shall remain mine through my dreams, the fragments of happiness that I had with you shall stay locked away for good. Let us make the most of it . . . and that shall be that. **Q**.

That shall be that? When, pray tell, shall the children visit me through *my* dreams? Are they are not as much mine as they are yours? **Purse**.

Weekends? **Q**.

And holidays. **Purse**.

Holidays? I think not! I shall have my lawyer Jack Brenner iron out the details. **Q**.

Do that. And while you're at it, have him tear down that hideous red picket-fence! **Purse**.

I take back what I said about the house. I want to keep it through my own memories. It is no longer yours! **Q**.

You bastard! I put just as much dreamy thought into that house as you! **Purse**.

And the rose bushes. I want those back as well. **Q**.

Mr. Q Train, my name is David Knight and I am Miss Purse's attorney. You get no imaginary rose bushes. And you get no imaginary house. Leave the dreamy thoughts to Miss Purse before this gets messy. **Knight**.

Mr. Knight, my name is Jack Brenner and I am Mr. Q Train's attorney. Messy? You haven't seen messy. You know full well that this fantasy house is just as much my client's as yours! **Brenner**.

I know nothing, except that my client is not getting a fair deal. I shall see you in court. **Knight**.

And I shall see *you* in court! **Brenner**.

See you there! **Knight**.

Saw you on the Q train, late afternoon, June 12. You were wearing a red dress, carrying a black purse. You have officially been served. Respond here. **Brenner**.

Never done this before. Am counter-suing. Now what? Let it begin, my love. *Let it begin!* **Purse**.

Outsourcing My Love

Dearest, Most Wonderful Darling:

I write this letter with all the hope of Vishnu and all the essence of Brahma in pronouncing that today is the very best day in the history of the entire universe! That is how much I think today is the best day in forever and ever!

Ekam sat, Viprah Bahudha vadanti!

I know, I know! You are bored by such a tired cliché, but may I give you the pleasure of my uttering once more its full translation?

That which is the sole truth, the wise (and by implication the unwise) call by many names.

The truth. That is why I am writing to you today, my dearest, most wonderful darling! Not as your husband. Not as your lover. Not even as a friend. Not even with my own hand. In another's hand. A stronger, more capable hand. Hence the fancy handwriting that you may not quite recognize. Also, the odd, exotic postmark to be found on the Air-Mail envelope from India from whence this letter was dispatched. And the aforementioned reference to Vishnu and Brahma. I write this love letter, via proxy, from a distance, while on vacation with my company, and with all of my heart and soul. Which is a far more difficult task. And expensive. But more meaningful! I outsource my love for you halfway across the world! *This* is how much I love you!

Do not cry with happiness, my lover! I have so much more that I would like to now tell you, via this Indian expert's thoughts in my first-person voice, on this, my first love letter to you in over 15 years, as I play golf in Bermuda while on a company retreat that is both unavoidable and much regrettable, but necessary.

Let me further explain: I have taken the liberty of jotting down a few of the specifics that mean the most to me about our beautiful relationship, in general terms, and then forwarding it to the gentleman who now writes the letter that you currently hold in your no-doubt trembling hands. (I think, but cannot fully remember, that the name of this letter writer is Suku.

Regardless, he promised me, with all of his honor, that he would perform this enviable task with a strong dose of conviction—just after the check successfully cleared. I can only trust that he is a man of his word.)

But enough about me. Allow me now, through Suku, to write of you! Where to begin? Let me start with your lips, as red as a sunset rising over the Himalayas at dawn and more moist than the steam hissing off the great River Ganges! I do not exaggerate! But why stop there? You are, indeed, the most gorgeous woman on *any* continent, India's or otherwise. For millions of kilometers around, there is no one to beat your beauty! And that goes for North America, where you reside.

One cannot deny, my darling, that we have had some wonderful times over the years, yes? Do you remember that weekend when we both traveled on vacation? Or when we mutually took a long drive and enjoyed each other's company? What else? The walks. The lovemaking sessions. The dinners. The lunches. And the other meals, including the occasional champagne brunch. I could go on and on, but I shan't.

Let me, by way of Suku, digress. Can you recall the scene in the classic 1971 movie *Lakshminarasimha*, in which the main character puts down his plate of moong pani, cleans off his thick, black beard, and then roars with joyous laughter, as the women around him fling rose petals and proceed to dance? Of course you can! That is how I now feel! I am laughing and laughing and laughing—and I can only assume that you are laughing as well! Or are you convulsing with joy and delight?

Do not feel the need to answer. But if you must, please feel free (after paying the appropriate postage) to send return correspondence to the address listed on the back of this fancy, pink, perfumed envelope from whence this letter was sent. Please allow between four to six weeks for a response, six to eight if you wish it to be detailed.

And yet, my darling, this love of which Suku now writes through my first-person voice is not all about Indian musk roses or laughing with joy at those who dance the bharatanatyam around you. It is also about other things, far more important things! May I once again borrow one of our favorite sayings?

*Avidyam antare vartamanah svayam dhirah
panditam manyamanah jagghanya manah
pariyanti mudha andhenaiva niyamana yatha
'ndhah.*

Okay, okay! You have heard me utter this pearl one million times, plus one! And it is no mystery, as you know, that this gem is translated as follows:

Abiding in the midst of ignorance, thinking themselves wise and learned, fools go aimlessly hither and thither, like blind led by the blind.

Blind. How could I, as your lover, have waited so long to hire another man on another continent to write you the love letter that you have so often tenderly requested? Laziness, too much time spent at work, boredom, not knowing a whole lot about India—these are mere excuses! I was wrong! And foolish! Which is why I am praying that this missive will remedy any lack of attention that I might have exhibited over the years for a woman with eyes the color of the black marble at Humayun's Tomb and with hair the shade of the golden sand on the Marari Beach that is located in the southwest Kerala town of Alleppey, roughly 3,000 kilometers (or 1864.113 miles) from Nassau, Bahamas, where I vacation, as you tend to our three children, six dogs, and one partially deaf transfer student.

In short, my darling, I love you, by another man's dreams, hopes, and thoughts, more than life itself; a love that I could never, ever!, come close to capturing on paper—especially by way of another's most honorable, exotic, brown hands.

**With warmest affection
and from "The 19th Hole Restaurant,"**

Your Dearest Husband

/suku patel

IKEA Instructions

1

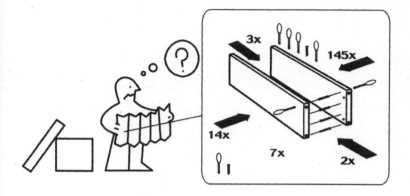

2

3

4

5

6

7

8

9

10

11

12

13

14

15

Dear Mister Thomas Pynchon

(A Rhon Penny Letter)

Dear Mister Thomas Pynchon:

Thank you for taking the time to open this envelope and read what is contained herein. I know that you, like me, are a very busy and serious man, so I don't intend to waste our times.

I will have you know that while I am a fan of your work, this is the first instance in which I have attempted to make contact with you. You could say that I was waiting for the exact right moment and, if you did say that, then you would be right.

I am a writer named Rhon Penny (silent *h*), and I am
no longer married. I am writing to you today because I
have just finished my latest novel, and it would be my
great honor for you to blurb it. If you are unaware, a
blurb is one of those glowing remarks you find on the
back of a book's cover, written by a highly regarded
author or TV chef. For example, if I were blurbing this
letter, it would go:

*"If you could only read two things this year, make one
this letter . . . and the other maybe the* Magna Carta*!"*

In today's literary climate, it is essential that a new
writer obtain a blurb so that Joe Q. Dumbbell thinks a
book is worthy enough of purchase or library checkout.
My publisher/mother tells me a top-notch blurb can
mean the difference between Harry Potter-type sales
and Harry Stottleberg-type sales (a guy who lives in
our building). As my primary-care physician says,
"Humans are fickle pickles," which, while true, has never
really explained why he has me on such a complicated
smorgasbord of pharmaceuticals. I am very tired.

Like yourself (no doubt) I find blurbing to be absolutely
repulsive. It is crass, pathetic, and couldn't be less
artistic. Just so you know, I am only doing this because
the more I think about it, the more I would like to make
a lot of money. Full disclosure: I named my conjoined
Siamese cats Tommy and Pinchie. Tommy just died,
which has made movement difficult for Pinchie. But she
pushes on like a feline boat against the current, borne
back ceaselessly into the past (F. Scott Fitzgerald).

Like blurbs, an author's choice of title is very important
for sales. Take *Gravity's Rainbow*. That is a terrific

title. Why? Because it tells you exactly what the book is about. I would like to think that my book's title does the same: *Cream of America Soup*.

Okay. By this point, I am going to assume that you have already agreed to blurb me, so let me just say, "Thank you." I truly appreciate it.

Let us now concentrate on the blurb itself. If you would like to construct your own blurb, then, please, by all means, construct it! You're good with words. On the other hand, should you prefer that I create a blurb for you to affix your name and well-deserved reputation to, then I have taken the liberty of coming up with some samples (please note the use of exclamation points).

Here they are:

> *"Fifteen thumbs up!"*

> *"If I had a disease that made me retch every time I read a great sentence, I would never stop vomiting while reading Ron Penny's latest novel!"* [Note the misspelling of "Rhon." This will get people talking.]

> *"It is not for me to say whether Rhon Penny is a great new young talent, but I will say this: Yes, he is greatly talented, and no, he is not young!"*

> *"If I were married to Rhon Penny . . . I would never leave him!"*

You have to be wondering: What in the world is this novel I've agreed to blurb actually about? And why is Rhon no longer married? Excellent queries both. I will not tell you why I'm no longer married, but my book's subject matter is very much like *Gravity's Rainbow* in a way, and in other ways not at all. It's also very much a post-9/11 book, but not overtly. I'm not saying you need to know a lot about the medieval feudal system, Lady Bird Johnson, bats, my ex-wife's fear of conjoined Siamese cats, democracy, or linguini . . . but it wouldn't be such a bad thing if you did.

What I *am* saying, however, is that the book takes place in Connecticut. (Yes, I am aware that a lot of people refuse to write about the Nutmeg State—for obvious reasons—but it is a state I know and care deeply about. Furthermore, being afraid of criticism just ain't in Rhon's genetic makeup.)

For reasons I can't get into, I must immediately end this correspondence. But I will not sign off without addressing the giant elephant in this letter. Yes, if you blurb my book I will then blurb your next one. And I can promise you, as sure as I'm writing this letter with my lucky Bic pen, that it will be laudatory . . . even if I absolutely hate it! I just have a funny feeling that I'm going to "adore" and "love" and "highly recommend" the thing! Catch my "drift"?

In closing, let me say three things. One, I would certainly take my ex-wife back if she ever leaves Bernard. Two, feel free to keep the enclosed sign that reads "Danger! Writer's Zone!" That is a gift and it will go well in your office. And three, please allow me to express what I have to say in the form of a blurb:

"If you could grow great people in the ground like tomatoes, then I would only plant seeds of you in the garden of my life so that I could have you available

to top all of my future life-salads. That said, if you could send a really well-thought-out blurb to my return address, I would greatly appreciate it!"

Self-addressed envelope included. Stamps not, but highly recommended.

Yours in the words,
Rhon Penny

My Name Is Smokey

Hi! My name is Smokey. I am a five-year-old, black-and-white collie, male, with blue eyes and a very sweet personality. I have lived with my current owner since I was a pup, but unfortunately I need to find a new forever home because my owner's situation has changed. I am a very well-behaved doggy: friendly, neutered, super-lovable, and 100 percent disease and demon-free!

Can you make room in your home for a furry, happy, loving, "non-traditional" dog like me? I sure hope so!

I'm okay living in a small space. My previous owner's space was a tiny two-bedroom house, but my owner had to leave the premises in kind of a hurry. I love long walks that don't pass churches or religious-affiliated cemeteries, and I'm a fiend for the dog run. I shouldn't be around babies, goats, or home-constructed altars, and I love to nap on a big fat pillow!

I've learned lots of tricks. I can catch, play dead, beg, shake hands, and levitate. I'm a big talker. I can bark once for "please," and if you give me a snack you'll get two barks for "thank you." Recently, I've also learned to bark in what may sound like Latin or ancient Sumerian. But don't worry. It's not like a demonologist once attempted to rid a malevolent presence from my owner's house by trapping the demon in my body. I'm just a wacky, woofy doggy!

Speaking of wacky woofing, you should know that I'm one of those dogs who starts to resemble the family he's with. That's why it may sound as if the voice of your deceased grandmother or other long-lost relative is coming out of my cute mouth, but that's just Smokey being Smokey! It's definitely not Smokey being a conduit for the netherworld!

My coat is long and it will need a lot of brushing! But don't even worry about fleas! The only wingless critters you'll need to worry about are the hordes of scuttling fanged crabs that come to play with me during the vernal equinox.

I have a few dietary requirements. Like lots of dogs of my breed, I'm really not a fan of store-bought dog food. Call me spoiled, but lately I will only eat food from animals that were slaughtered before my eyes, preferably with a knife carved from onyx. I also love it when my din-din's entrails are wrapped in 16th-century Hungarian crushed-velvet silk and buried at the easternmost point of your lawn. I'm a picky doggy!

Additionally, I should never be allowed to eat clover or sage. *Ever.* Eating clover or sage will make me feel like I have a grumbly tummy, and that I'm surging with the invincible power of the dark armies of Nysrogh, so keep that stuff away from me!

(Seriously, if you have sage or clover in your garden it has to be removed. This can't be stressed enough. Set your garden plots on fire and then pave over them with concrete, just to be sure. If I ever eat clover or sage, all I can say is things are going to get ruff, indeed!)

I have so much to offer! I have literally come out of my shell, and I am becoming more and more social. I am great with humans who cower before me, but cats and priests with wrong intentions just make me angry! I will cool down quickly if I am placed gently onto a throne and then carried through town on the backs of four middle-aged virgin men. I am also prone to motion sickness.

Before adopting me, my new mommy and daddy should know that I have not finished growing just yet! I am a medium-size doggie who is getting larger and larger every day and who has not yet reached his ultimate height of nine-and-a-half feet. I hungry!

I almost always come when called, but if you're ever shouting for me and I'm being stubborn, try calling me by my nickname, "Baalzephon, Leader of the Foot Soldiers for Hell's Army." Just be sure to never call me by my nickname three times in a row, or while staring into a mirror. And definitely never call me by my nickname while you're menstruating.

Do you have the patience to raise a differently-abled pooch? Then I may be the one for you! Here's a question: Can't some doggies be a little special and have between their legs a birch rod to mete out punishment instead of a boring ol' tail?

I hope I'm not sounding like one of those high-maintenance doggies! Though I need a little extra care, I'm just a regular lovable pup who is definitely not possessed by the spirit of the second captain of Hades' sentinels. And even if I was, it's just because my owner's demonologist promised she could cleanse his house by pouring the evil spirits into my pretty furry body, but the demonologist never told him what was going to happen for the rest of eternity. Besides, if you ever feel the need to know if I have any demons inside me, you just have to go get some help from a demonologist who's still alive.

Piece of cake!

I'm ready to move in today! Just come and get me from the corner of Palmer and Landvale. You will know it because it's the only house on the block that was recently swallowed up by the ground below. You'll find me sitting in the middle of the sunken plot, waiting ever so patiently. Do you want me to come home with you? All you have to do is look me directly in the eye and say,

"Rise, Baalzephon! You are welcome to my home, and I am humbled to subject myself wholly to thine rule!"

Easy peasy!

My name is Smokey and I can't wait to join your happy happy family!!! Won't you give this remarkable doggy a chance?

A Short Story Geared to College Students, Written by a Thirtysomething Author

"Frat Party Blues: Rockin' It, Fort Lauderdale Style!"

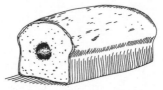

"What up, chief?" asked Larry. He had just finished soccer practice, and was now sucking back on a bottle of his favorite brew, 40-Dog Buzz.

"Nothing, friend," said Charles.

Larry and Charles had been best buds for three years now. And Charles knew absolutely *everything* about Larry, including Larry's intense hunger for "vagina."

"How was math class?" asked Charles, trying to get Larry's goat. "Did you study for that test?"

"Fuck off, bitch!" said Larry. "You know damn well that I didn't study for that test. What in the fuck?"

"Easy, friend," said Charles. "Just take it easy. I was only kidding."

Larry laughed, as he knew that Charles was merely being facetious. "So . . . are you planning on attending that party tonight?" he continued.

"Fuck yes," answered Charles. "And I plan to stick my penis into a loaf of bread. It should be kickin'.'"

"Just like last time," said Larry.

Now it was Charles's turn to laugh. After he finished, he said: "Better yet, how about that frat party we learned about on the World Wide Web? The one taking place in Florida? I'm thinking road trip."

Larry thought for a minute, and then replied: "'Cause I'm thinking the same! Let's do it. And let's invite Janet!"

Larry gave Charles the high five, and then climbed into his tremendous Sport Utility Vehicle, or S.U.V., complete with the most amazing stereo sound system in the world.

"Kick out the jams, motherfucker!" screamed Charles from the passenger's seat.

Larry did as he was asked, and within no time, Limp Bizkit [sic] was blasting from the nine Bose speakers and seven specialized subwoofers that Larry had installed the previous month. The sound was absolutely monstrous.

Larry and Charles gave each other another high five, and then sped off through the university's front gates to Janet's house in the western, and more fancy, part of town.

Janet was already waiting for them. She looked ravenous: extremely tight shorts, blue tank top, open-toe sandals, breasts (soft and large) swinging to and fro. Exquisite.

"What's the story, boys?" Janet asked, climbing into the backseat of the S.U.V., but not before Larry caught a quick glimpse of her tremendous right nipple.

Larry, Charles, and Janet had been friends forever. She treated them like brothers, and they, in turn, treated her like a sister. A sister whose image they could fantasize about and then later, when it was dark, masturbate to.

"Nothin'," said Charles, taking a swig from his freshly opened bottle of brewsky. "Just high-tailin' it down to Florida. For a little of this and that."

"Sweet," said Janet, absentmindedly stroking her sweaty tank top. "Freakin' sweet."

☆ ☆ ☆

It was a few hours later and Charles, Larry, and Janet were walking down the main avenue of Fort Lauderdale, searching for the frat house that they had read about on The Internet.

"Is that the house?" asked Janet. She was now wearing a pink bikini, flip-flops, and a shark's-tooth necklace, the latest fashion rage.

"Don't think so," said Larry, popping open some fresh suds. He offered some to Charles, who refused, on account of the marijuana joint he had just lit up.

"I'm so high that I could fly," said Charles, taking a puff. "The world is all about colors and love and freedom."

Larry and Janet laughed. It was nothing to see one of their friends "high," but this was ridiculous!

"You could touch the moooooon!" said Janet, now absentmindedly pulling at her bathing-suit top. "You're *that* high!"

"Yo, easy, bitch!" said Charles. And then: "Just kiddin'."

Janet took no offense—she was used to such behavior from Charles. And besides, "bitch" was a term of endearment when used among friends and close acquaintances.

"Where in the fuck is this party?" asked Larry, growing frustrated. "Brother, I could really use some vagina."

"Easy, chooch," replied Charles, pointing to a large, all-glass house situated directly on the beach. "There it is. The answer to all of our dreams."

Larry and Janet looked up at the same time. The frat house was *beautiful*. Just like Charles had said: all-glass and situated directly on the beach. It could not have been more magnificent!

Larry, Charles, and Janet nervously walked up the white concrete driveway to the front door. When they reached it, Larry pressed the doorbell. A song rang out. It sounded like "Californication" by the very popular funk-and-soul group Red Hot Chili Peppers, but they could not be sure.

"May I help you?" asked a deep and throaty voice from behind the tremendous solid-oak door. "This is a private fraternity party. No outsiders allowed!"

Larry and Charles looked at each other. *Shit*, they thought. *Fucking shit.*

"Just kiddin'," said the deep voice, as the door opened to reveal a gorgeous older woman dressed in a black cocktail dress, stilettos, and a gold-chain necklace. Letting her voice rise to its normal level, she said: "I don't always talk like that. Hi, my name is Nancy. And I'm 26."

Goddamn the monkey man! thought Larry. And then, aloud: "May we come in?"

"Right this way," answered Nancy, leading all three into the grand foyer. She then spread her arms wide: "Welcome, dear friends from a distant state!"

What Janet, Charles, and Larry observed next absolutely amazed them, stunning them beyond belief:

> *Pyramids, 15 feet high, created with only empty beer cans!*

> *Smoke from marijuana cigarettes wafting toward the rafters above!*

> *Large fraternity types placing compact discs into compact-disc players!*

> *Half-naked women, their breasts jingling and jangling, perched on the shoulders of football players!*

> *Pizza pies, half-eaten, lazily strewn across expensive leather couches!*

> *A fat man with a beard pouring vodka into a crystal punch bowl!*

> *And a dog, lying amid all of this chaos, attempting to sleep.*

"Aw, spit!" exclaimed Larry. "This is the best fraternity party that I've ever seen!"

Charles could only nod. He agreed, but was too shocked to say anything.

Janet, on the other hand, could not stop talking: "This is incredible, absolutely incredible. I mean, I've always thought Florida parties were supposed to be delightful, but this . . . this . . . "

"Has all been *worth* it?" Charles asked.

Janet nodded, then began to weep.

Without another word, Larry, Charles, and Janet linked their arms together . . . and walked into the amazing, cacophonous fray.

☆ ☆ ☆

"Peace."

It was a few hours later and Charles was turning off his miniature cellular telephone and placing it back into his T-shirt pocket.

"That was Nancy," exclaimed Charles. "She wanted to thank us for coming to the party. There sure was a lot of wonderful vagina!"

Janet rolled her eyes. She was very tired and there were still many hours to travel before they arrived home. "Can't you just cool it? All I've heard since we've left the party is vagina this and vagina that. *Enough!*"

Charles and Larry laughed long and hard.

When they were finished, Larry asked: "What's the matter, bitch? Can't take the heat? Just kiddin'." He tapped the S.U.V.'s horn, which blasted out "Return of Saturn" by the No Doubt. He had it installed while he was down in Fort Lauderdale, and it was smokin'.

"Yes, I'll have you know," replied Janet, "that I can very much take the heat. It's just that I'm tired and could use some rest." She absentmindedly swiped at her sweaty left nipple and then at her right nipple, which was also sweaty.

"Easy, you two," said Charles, flicking on the tremendously powerful car stereo system and slapping in a Korn [*sic*] compact disc. "Time to bust out some kick-ass tunes!"

The ferocious alternative sounds of "Make Me Bad" filled the vehicle.

Larry popped open a cool one and then leaned back into the S.U.V.'s front passenger seat. The sun was starting to set and the air was beginning to grow chilly.

"Goodnight," said Janet, reclining into her comfy backseat. "See you when I see you."

"Until then," said Charles.

"On the other side," said Larry.

They gave each other the high five, and then Charles took another puff from his reefer.

College life is sweet, Larry thought, falling into a deep and gentle sleep. *So goddamn sweet that it was motherfuckin' ridiculous.*

Note: Mike Sacks is in his thirties. This is his first story about college students.

Signs Your College Is Not Very Prestigious

Your mascot is a tiger in a wheelchair

•

Most famous alumnus: the inventor of the "cheese inside the crust" pizza

•

Statue of university founder is in a fetal position

•

School advertises on urinal cakes

Orientation includes chemical delousing

•

Scholarships awarded via "Hottest Buns" contest

•

Offers a minor in "Winning Radio Contests"

•

Marching band uses only handclaps

•

Community-service requirement is handing out
half-off fliers in front of competing colleges

•

The college motto, translated from the Latin:
"To Dry Retch"

•

Faculty re-staffed daily by illegal immigrants
brought in by pick-up truck

•

Financial-aid package consists of $10 and
a pack of smokes

•

Has a swim-up dining hall

•

One robe passed from person to person in diploma line

Astronomy professor frequently forgets which
direction outer space is

•

Late fee assessed for diplomas held more than three days

•

Has NCAA's only cockfighting program

•

Desks in classrooms equipped with seat belts

•

Your meal plan is "24-Hour-All-You-Can-Eat
Hot Pockets"

•

The only required reading: *Don Diva* magazine

•

When you graduated "Cum Laude," the word "cum"
was written on your diploma in a sperm font

•

Every time you answer a question in class, the professor
says, "I guess you think you're better than me"

•

Provost walks around campus with a Burmese
python around his neck

•

The first time you brought a laptop to class,
the other students thought you were a time traveler
from the future

The dean has a reputation for being a bit of a "gash hound"

•

Big man on campus is a 700-pound shut-in

•

"Counseling Services" is a candy dish of Adderall

•

Valedictorians are determined by a mixed-martial-arts cage match

•

Doesn't have a campus radio station but does have its own CB-radio handle

•

The "grading couch"

Rules for My Cuddle Party

Hey, folks! Just a few points of interest before the fun begins:

#1. Please do not give birth in the hot tub. I only say as much because at my last cuddle party, a woman gave "natural" birth to a set of twins in the hot tub.

#2. I'd appreciate it if you didn't use my grandmother's hand-knitted pillows as an impromptu sex swing. I only bring this up because at my last cuddle party, a man by the name of "Doctor Pump" (nickname?) used my grandmother's knitted pillows as an impromptu sex swing.

#3. I'm the "lifeguard." That means I'm in charge. Whatever I say goes. When I drop this ostrich feather, that means it's officially time to begin. Also, if I tell you not to use my prescription psoriasis ointment as a sex lubricant, please don't. I only say this because at my last cuddle party, a group of teens from the local high school found their way into my medicine cabinet, climbed on top of my kitchen table, and then used my psoriasis ointment as a sex lubricant.

#4. Please do not frighten any of the neighbors, especially the easily startled 59-year-old with Asperger's and a propensity for speed-dialing the authorities. I'm telling you this because at my last cuddle party, a group of recently released prisoners (none of whom I had previously met, and who had only learned about my cuddle party from a mysterious pamphlet stapled to a lamppost across from a methadone clinic) loudly popped their "freedom cherries" beneath the bedroom window of my neighbor, the easily startled 59-year-old with a propensity for speed-dialing the authorities.

#5. I would love it if you did not urinate into my backyard air-conditioning compressor. I'm no Nostradamus, far from it, just an accountant, new to the area, whose only wish last weekend was to throw a cuddle party to meet some fantastic new friends and to create an alcohol- and drug-free environment where people could explore non-sexual touch and unlimited affection without being criticized. What I'm trying to say is that I'm definitely not the type of person who can somehow peak into the future and magically foresee that a woman, wearing only panties depicting Bugs Bunny with a large, gray erection, would (for whatever reason) show up at my house on a mini-motorbike, quickly become drunk off homemade strawberry wine, and then urinate into my backyard air-conditioning compressor.

#6. One last thing: can you please refrain from taking an oatmeal bath in my guest bedroom, even if you do happen to have a rash on your genitals? I hesitate to even bring this up, but at my last cuddle party—before the local TV news and a group of representatives from the Department of Health and Human Services broke down my front door—a dishwasher on his lunch break from the Original Spaghetti Factory snuck into my kitchen, stole a container of oatmeal, and then took a long, medicated soak in my guest bedroom, which just so happens to not contain a bathroom or a bathtub.

#7. Got it? Good! Actually, not good. SUPER!!! Because with that "official business" now out of the way, let's. Do. Some. Serious. Cuddlin'!!!!

**Your Official "Cuddle Party Lifeguard,"
Mike**

P.S.—*PLEASE* help yourself to the whitefish-and-egg-salad spread . . . Juicy Juice is also available, with exact change . . .

Geoff Sarkin Is Using Twitter!

Fixing bowtie. Last moment of freedom! Putting out cig, making sure breath doesn't smell . . . Ok! Let's get married!

Walking down aisle. Stopping. Family and friends waiting for me to finish update. Patience, people! And . . . done.

Yes! Yes, I DO take Helen to be my lawfully wedded wife! Rabbi, please respond when you receive this Tweet.

Also, confirm that it's wedded with two d's.

Two d's, right? Thought so. And we're good to go? Oh, yes, the kiss! LOL

Still LOLing.

Helen not laughing, maybe she will in a sec—

No, still not laughing.

Kiss is wonderful. Better than expected!

Attempting to fist-bump rabbi. He's nodding NO. Not cool! Now what? Anyone know where the receiving line is?

For those of you at the end of the line, yes it's really boring, I know! Orioles are losing, by the way. BIG surprise.

Ending receiving line early. To everyone still waiting: THANK YOU FOR TRYING. Send your good wishes to geoff.sarkin8@gmail.com

Attaching photo of Aunt Bess looking into camera phone telling me to put down camera phone. Not a bad shot, if I say so myself.

At reception now. Someone do me a kindness? Google "Wedding Dance + Instructions + 'Always on My Mind.'" Thx.

Uncle Bob from Australia came! Can't believe he flew 22 hours for this! Just after triple bypass!

Uncle Bob trying to talk to me. Sending u email, Uncle. Kind of busy now, obviously.

Can't see b/c Helen just smashed wedding cake in my face. Now have cake all over Iphone.

Not funny baby. Can't seem to use the exclamation point now

Now I can!!!!!!!!!!

Guests starting to leave. Check Facebook when you get home, people. Might just be a virtual bouquet of flowers waiting.

A little mass email to say, "I love u all, even if I did forget some of your names"

Checking in at hotel. It's ok, not great. Just kidding! It rocks! Good Iphone reception. Walking to room. Orioles lost, btw. SUCKS.

Alone at last! Luckily Blue Jays also lost! Watching video of our first wedding dance. Helen looks ravishing! See http://tinyurl. com/kvvw3g!

Thanks, Max, for taking over while I shot video!

Geoff Sarkin will be out of office until 2/27. He's on his honeymoon & not to be disturbed! Someone at work please post this on system tomorrow?

BTW, how did Beth in marketing do on her run last weekend? And what was flavor of the Friday donut?

Need to know ASAP! Don't care what time of night it is!!!!!!!!!!

Nude and waiting for wife to enter bed

Anyone see the repeat of *Law & Order* last night?

Would u rather be an elephant or a giraffe? I'd rather be a giraffe. Not sure why. They seem happy. Must be the size of the neck . . .

Wife getting into bed.

Oral sex has commenced. Taking off dress sock . . . and now the other . . .

Oral sex has commenced again.

Helen seems to be enjoying self. Anyone out there have any oral sex stories they care to share? They're usually pretty funny

Making love now. Check out this amazing article on the guy who invented wonton soup http://tinyurl.com/yftcny6

What's that part called again? Aireola? Eereola? Areola?

DAMN! JUST MY LUCK!!!!!!!!!!!!! I love double chocolate donuts! Ahhhhhhhhhhh! SAVE ONE!!!!!!!

Before I forget . . . Marnie, can you check to see if my computer is off?

Still making love

No change since last update.

Helen orgasming. I'm changing Facebook status to "Married."

Helen still going. Sending in-laws Facebook "poke." Important to maintain good relations

Ceiling shadows look like sea creatures! I take it back. Don't want to be giraffe. Def want to be sea creature! Cos they swim so fast?

Helen finished and off to bathroom

Helen brushing teeth.

Finishing my orgasm now—

Think I might hit the hay. Exhausted! Will check back in at 3 am everyone! Still thinking of sea creatures. What a day!

It IS Areola! Thought so. Thanks, Dad. Is it too soon to call you "dad"?

Uh oh. Having 2nd thoughts about marriage. Ha. JOKING! This is the best!

Nighty night everyone! Tweet y'all REAL soon . . .

Taking off bowtie now.

Reasons You're Still Single

You . . .

Own a 60-inch flat-screen plasma television,
but sleep on a broken futon

•

Have a ferret on your shoulder, and you're at the mall

•

Own tie-dyed gym clothes

•

Only feel truly alive in the Renaissance
Faire jousting area

Have your "lucky" anal beads hanging from
your rear-view mirror

•

List "Dungeonmaster" on your business card

•

Hug amusement-park mascots

•

Own a "It's Not Going to Suck Itself" T-shirt
and the "Not" has faded away

•

Will do anything for "shits and giggles"

•

Display with pride your framed degree from
drunk-driving school

•

Have a "Peeing Calvin" decal on your electric car

•

Perform yoga in parks

•

Have a dangerously high Thetan count

•

Bring your camera to Happy Hour

•

Sleep wearing only a shirt, Porky Pig–style

•

Refuse to drink any beer that has not been
"beachwood aged"

•

Can only make love while blasting "Orinoco Flow" by Enya

Favorite pickup line: "Hi, I once beat to death
an elderly deaf man."

•

Have taken a date to a restaurant with license plates
and antique rakes on the walls

•

Consider yo-yo tricks a wonderful way to break the ice

•

Define wearing an umbrella hat as your "calling card"

•

Carry an NPR *Fresh Air* tote bag

•

Have a screen saver of yourself posing with
your Frisbee-golf bros

•

Believe the mouth is self-cleaning

•

Proudly display a Winnie the Pooh flag

•

Initiate wedding line-dances

•

Own the complete trilogy of *Benji* novelizations

•

Steadfastly refuse to remove that birthmark
in the shape of a swastika

•

Scream out *Wheel of Fortune* answers

•

Own slot-machine gloves

Emulate the fashion sense exhibited by the
Rastafarian culture

•

Refer to your penis as "Da Mayor"

•

Purchased your dining-room set using "Marlboro Miles"

•

Have an essentially unattractive appearance
and/or personality

Opening Lines to the Rough Draft of Rudyard Kipling's "If"

If you can keep your head when all about you

Are losing theirs

Are losing theirs

Are

?

Shit.

Lord.

Losing their arms?

Sanity?

Ink in pen?

Ok.

Fresh start.

Party on Sat.

Peanut butter.

Crackers.

Soda water maybe.

Fun balloons?

Ok.

Fresh start.

If you can keep your head when all about you

Are losing theirs

Are losing theirs

Are

If you can keep your head when all about you, when all

about you, when, if you can, if, all about you,

Screw it.

Dr. Margaret MacLeod:

Daydream Tutor

No, you cannot leave, Benjamin! Grab your sippy cup and mount your imaginary horse! There's a macho cowboy! Watch for the scalp hunters!

You asked me what I do for a living and I'm going to tell you: I teach kids how to daydream. You're shaking your head. Don't. Actually, at one time I was just like you: "Now why do you have to teach daydreaming? Aren't kids capable of that already?" What can I say? I didn't invent daydreaming, I'm just perfecting it. *There we go, Tabitha! Just ease up on the trembling, sweetie! I like that! You're Maria in* The Sound of Music! *Here come the Nazis!* She gets nervous.

So what else can I tell you? You want a story? A mother barges into the studio [Daydream Believin', Intersection of Falls and River Roads], she's frantic. This was sometime around April. "Help! My boy's about to turn eight, doesn't know how to daydream, all of his friends can daydream, he's losing weight, depressed, etc.!" I was calm and I was soothing: "Honey, it is never too late! Let's just see what your child can accomplish . . ."

Oooh boy, he was atrocious! Couldn't think of a decent adventure to save his life. You should see him now! One of my better students, I have hundreds. *Peter, put on your space helmet and fly yourself to the moon!* He's practicing hard for national competition in a few weeks. *Blastoff is in five seconds . . . uh oh. Explosion!* The way he's crying, you'd think he really was going to Mars. . . .

You wouldn't believe the pressure these kids are under! Dear Lord, I am serious! I'm just throwing a name out, but little Zachory grows up and before he knows it, he's in the third grade and not keeping up with his classmates. So who are you then going to turn to? Yourselves? Do you have the necessary guidance skills? Not a chance. . . .

Zachory, you're the world's richest surgeon! Uh oh! Your patient just stopped breathing! You have five seconds to fix the situation! Cool!

I came to daydreaming late. I was studious and never had the time. But I have always enjoyed observing the daydreamers around me, they've fascinated me—except for my husbands! Did I always know I'd be good at this? Truthfully, yes. I felt the calling—

He's dead, Zachory. Move on to the next patient.

But did I ever sit back and think: Hooray, the kids are out of the house at last! The divorce [settlement] check has finally been cashed! And now at my slightly advanced age, ahem, I can at last devote myself full-time to the art of daydreaming? Probably not— *Rachel, keep your eyes closed when you float down that imaginary stream! Do not fall into old habits! Uh oh. Here comes the giant piranha.* Like many things in my life, it just happened.

Robert, make way for the flying witches! Do not shake your head! I am not one of your pals!

The future of daydreaming? It's limitless. I'd love to open a studio in every single city across the country. I have a waiting list as long as my arm. Parents love it here. By the way, have you seen my instruction manuals? Aren't they marvelous?

THE WITCHES! DUCK!

If they had covers, would you ever have guessed they were self-published? I also wrote the blurbs. Would you like to buy a few copies? Maybe next time. . . .

Nighttime daydreaming, who's ready? The monster is out and he. Is. HUNGRY!

So thanks for stopping by, and do me a favor: on your way out, hit the switch for the moon and the stars? *All of you, concentrate! It's the starriest night in history! But what's that? Is the moon about to explode?* There's a helper. Bye now.

From the Sea Journal
of the Esteemed
Dr. Ridley L. Honeycomb

(On Board His Majesty's Sloop *Winslow*)

May 3, 1804

First patient—a ruddy-faced seaman of nineteen.
Strong in spirit; most powerful. Complaint: stomach
distress. A fever that stubbornly refuses to subside.
"How are you handling the disquietness of the first few
days shipboard?" I ask. "Most honorably," he responds.
"That makes me glad," I counter. "Please, good surgeon,
may I request an elixir to relieve me of my discomfort?"
This uttered by the lad, through clenched teeth. At this,
I can only smile. Naïve youth!

Wordlessly, and with pipe in hand, I motion to the framed *PhD. in Psychology* certificate on the wall. "You are no fine surgeon?" he asks, somewhat plaintively.

I aid him to his feet with: "Worry not, good boy! We have months to sort this through." The young man eventually retreats, a little the worse for wear, true. But—one can only assume . . . more *sound* of mind?

May 6

Attacked by a Napoleonic frigate! Thirty-five wounded; nine unlucky men banished from this good earth. The screams, you can only imagine! The rivers of blood, only in your most frightful nightmares envision! So many injured, so much unhappiness! "You must help us, good Doctor!" they cry, almost in unison. "Help starts *here!*" I shout in response and I point to my head & heart.

Yes, they turned away in disappointment and pain, but (as with the sea itself) much work is done 'neath the surface.

May 15

"My arm! 'Tis severed!" This from our valiant Captain Jenkins, pinned 'neath the formidable weight of a fallen topgallant mast . . .

Said I: "May we converse a bit upon this dilemma?"

And he: "My arm . . . she is no more!"

And I: "Would you care to express your distress through a penciled rendering of this predicament? Here—with your *good* hand . . ."

As I now recline in my hammock, sipping sunflower-blossom tea and observing, with both wonder and joy, the stars that guide us toward our eventual destination (westward, I imagine), I cannot help but ponder how I might have handled such a ticklish situation differently: less severe love? More? New breathing exercises pilfered from my colleagues in the Orient?

I then think back fondly on similar, hypothetical cases from graduate school, minus the severed arms and fallen masts. Life is indeed deliciously humorous when arriving full course!

P.S.—The captain perished.

May 26: *Saturday*

More progress (and humour!) today. Assist'd the men in loading guano onto the vessel. Men complain of numbness in hands from such hard labour. When I counter with a deeper and more complex rationale (repressed rage over Mother's spankings), they laugh as if the mighty ocean Herself just passed gas. What foolishness we enjoy together! Good opening for future academic article? Thesis to come.

May 29

We are down to eighteen tired and disenchanted souls, and I thus find myself as lone commander. Trust Games 'neath the mizzen staysail at high noon. . . .

June 4

Down to sixteen men. Officers Wilson and Barrett did not take kindly to "Falling Backwards & Being Caught By Another." (Must pay special attention to Boundary Issues at upcoming Talk Circle assembly.)

Aug. 4: *Friday*

Pirates! The devil sweeps over us all! Buccaneers have overtaken our vessel! And most quickly! We are to be put to death at dawn's earliest light! Or perhaps by early afternoon. Maybe by nightfall. Possibly another time. Why am I forever doubting myself? Go with the first instinct . . . 'tis healthier!

Nightfall

A breakthrough of sorts with Arthur, the one-eyed leader of these imperfect, noble rogues. So much has been learnt over the course of our fifty-minute hour together . . . and yet (and as always) it comes down to all matters pertaining to the Sexual. In Arthur's case: impotence brought upon by the shame of his empty orbital cavity. I proffer that this phenomenon has less to do with his absent eye and more to do with the elderly shoe cobbler Arthur spoke about earlier in Group—the creepy one from the village over. The chap with the wandering hands and the "third peg leg." Positive changes begin now! Be gone with that off-putting eye patch, Arthur!!!

Later

Arthur returns to show me he has removed the "shame spiral" eye patch. In its stead: a gaping wound that is most disgusting to look at . . . it sickens and nauseates me. I wish to gag! It is beyond nature and outside the realm of what we consider "human"! And yet (and most impossibly) I consider this an *invaluable* first step. . . . Huzzah, Arthur!

Later Still

Still gagging. Back goes the eye patch and not quickly enough. A lesson of sorts: one must sometimes go with the *second* instinct . . . 'tis often better-considered.

August 7: Morn'

Glorious life & all she has to offer! A gusty storm raged for the entire Evening! All intrepid souls driven overboard into the Sea's ferocious churn . . . my new friend Arthur sadly included. Now I stand alone but not lonely.

First order of business will be to complete academic paper: "To Survive Without the Benefit of Adequate/Fresh Water, Food, Sanity." (Thesis to come.)

Second order of business: To replace objectionable pirate flags with more *inspirational* offering:

WARNING! LOVE IS THE ONLY FORCE CAPABLE OF TRANSFORMING AN ENEMY INTO A FRIEND! ALL ABOARD THE SMILE SHIP!!!!

I am the esteemed Dr. Ridley L. Honeycomb, PhD. . . . navigating the Sea of Hostility in search of the Land of Eternal Hope . . . and the horizon that dances, much like the incandescent butterfly that has just landed on my nose, shall soon be mine for the taking! This butterfly speaks! And it has much to say! And I am here to listen! . . .

Westward (I think). *Most optimistically!*

What in the Hell Is That Thing?

FAQ

The following questions were posed by you, my co-workers. Rather than answer them individually, I'll do so collectively. I apologize if your specific question wasn't picked, there were simply too many *excellent* ones to choose from . . .

1. What in god's name is that thing in the hallway? I noticed it upon my arrival at the office this morning. I'm frightened. Are you responsible?

Yes, but no need to be frightened! It's just a project I've been working on that should be finished any day now.

For the past few weeks I've had it conveniently hidden away in the storage room next to the elevator shaft, but it no longer fits. Hence its new location.

2. It's very large and disturbing. It pulses and beeps and hisses. It also emits a strange, noxious odor. Is it a sculpture of some kind? A machine? A robot?

Yes, it's a robot. But for the time being I'm just calling it "Untitled Project #1."

3. Who are you?

Merely a temp, hired to work in the reception area, answering the phones and greeting visitors. Supporting my inventor's way of life, doing my thing.

4. I've heard a rumor that you've been sleeping overnight here in the office. True?

If it's okay with all of you, I'd like to limit this FAQ to the robot . . .

5. When I got to work yesterday, I found a pillow and a blanket in my cubicle. Are you responsible? If so, why?

Okay, okay! I'm currently between "real" apartments and for the past few weeks, yes, I've been staying overnight here in the office, sleeping beneath various desks or on top of piles of your work. I do love it here. I've been tapping into a creativity that I didn't know previously existed. I love the emptiness. I love the feeling that I'm the only one in the world. I love foraging for "found objects" to make my masterpiece bigger and better. I love watching TV in the break room and taking leisurely strolls to get the creative juices flowing. The cleaning crew doesn't seem to mind.

6. That robot's preventing me from getting to my desk! It's taking up the entire hallway! Can I move it?

DO NOT TOUCH IT! It's very sensitive to outside stimuli! Have you touched it? If so, walk slowly backwards and preferably out of the building. Don't even think about the robot! (And don't pretend to leave and then come back. It'll know.) If you do confront it again, prostrate yourself before it. That seems to make it the most content.

7. How long will you be sticking around?

At least until June, when Leslie returns from maternity leave.

8. Will you take that monstrosity with you?

I hope so—I'd hate to leave it behind! On the other hand, I wouldn't dare try to "cut it down" and haul it out—it seems to have taken a liking to its new home.

9. I just discovered a tunnel leading from the men's bathroom into a large, cavernous space hidden between the walls. It almost looks like it's being turned into an apartment or laboratory of

some kind—as if someone will soon be moving in. Was this your doing?

Again, I hate to be rude, but I'd like to limit this FAQ to the robot, thanks.

10. The robot is now rocking back and forth. It looks angry. It's spitting out some type of viscous liquid. Should it be doing that?

Wow, that's a new one. A red liquid? Or a yellow liquid? Probably doesn't matter either way, as I don't know what the liquid is. This is my first robot. All this is novel for me too!

11. I have no question, per se. I just wanted to inform you that the robot is starting to speak.

Is it telling you that if you don't feed it, it'll kill you? Try Pop-Tarts from the snack machine. That worked for me the other night.

12. Bolts of lightning are shooting out of the robot's eyes! The robot is attacking the marketing department. The robot is flying around and around in circles. It has a buzzsaw on its side!

Yes, I am obviously aware of that. I'll attempt to "tweak" these and other problems after the office clears out for the evening. In other words, I'll do it when I can think . . . and when I'm not bothered with any major distractions, such as answering the phone or your queries.

13. I think I already know the answer to this, but will you sic the robot on us if we force you to leave?

Yes.

14. So you're telling us that everybody should just go back to work and carry on as normal? Are you mad?

About as mad as any "student of the universe" who's just created an invention-for-the-ages out of computer scraps and scavenged office supplies. Anyway, it's time for lunch, and I'm off to grab some lotto tickets and strips of turkey jerky.

15. This thing has cornered me in my office and is now screaming my name in what sounds like a violent, otherworldly language. I'm scared.

Ha! It's certainly not shy, I can tell you that! I don't know, wave at it or something. By the way, in my downtime, I also create handcrafted, artisan jewelry. Might make for the perfect gift?! I've taken the liberty of leaving a catalog on my desk. See you in a few!

—"Andrew in Reception"

The Three Laws of Robotics According to Isaac Asimov

Plus Twenty-One According to Me

1. A robot may not injure a human being.

2. A robot must obey the orders given it by human beings except where such orders would conflict with the First Law.

3. A robot must protect its own existence as long as such protection does not conflict with the First or Second Law.

4. A robot may not grow pubic hair.

5. A robot must never, under any circumstances, scat fresh lyrics to "Too-Ra-Loo-Ra-Loo-Ra."

6. A robot must never look at me as I balance my assorted chakras in any one of my numerous homemade beanbag chairs.

7. A robot must not maim, nor kill, me in an uncomfortable fashion after I patiently declare: "Are you not familiar with Law #6? Eyes elsewhere, thank you."

8. A robot must apologize for even thinking of maiming or killing me. A robot must then lift me onto its hard, stainless-steel back, and walk me over to the nearest IHOP for pancakes and coffee and, perhaps, just maybe, please dear Lord, a satisfying conversation about life, love, and loneliness.

9. A robot must always cook me delicious, low-fat meals (high in taste, low in calories), but only if said robot does not use milk or a milk product. (Important! I am lactose-intolerant.)

10. A robot, by law, must never be allowed to obtain a bartending degree through the mail.

11. If a robot does happen to obtain a bartending degree through the mail, this robot shall be turned off, covered in a burlap bag, driven to a farm on the outskirts of town, and then thrown out of the rear window of a speeding automobile or van.

12. If this robot does, for whatever reason, happen to find its way back home, said robot must be beaten severely with a large stick and broom and then tossed into the rear of a delivery truck, where it will then be driven to a farm on the opposite side of town.

13. If this robot still returns, pour maple syrup into its gear shaft. "Sorry," you will say. "You are powerful and I respect that, but really, you must now die."

14. A robot must mock any urologist or gynecologist who wears a Snoopy tie to put their patients at ease.

15. A robot must never trust a waiter who kneels when reciting the day's specials.

16. A robot must not make self-deprecating jokes with a fake foreign accent regarding its inability to bend over and touch its metallic toes.

17. When passing a homeless person with a "TELL ME OFF FOR $1" sign, a robot must always refrain from mentioning the obvious.

18. A robot must never go west to make it as a Hollywood star.

19. If said robot does attempt to go west to make it as a Hollywood star, this robot must be bound in rope, tied to the top of a limousine, and then driven to the set of a WB sitcom, where it must then—whether it wants to or not—audition for the role of "Put-upon Robot."

20. Sample dialogue:

Malcolm: "Pass the mustard, please."

Robot: "Sure, let me just adjust my pants first. This belt, it's a little loose."

(Laughter)

Eddie: "Typical robot! Always tightenin' their belts!"

(Tremendous laughter. Applause.)

21. A robot must always wash its hands after cleaning my ankle-length booties and before fixing me a tomato-and-cucumber sandwich, my absolute fave.

22. A robot must never bowl to the accompaniment of disco music or wear flip-flops on public transportation.

23. A robot must never flash gang signs while posing for wedding photos or give shout-outs to fellow robots.

24. Finally: A robot must love me with all its heart, with all of its soul, even if I am sometimes difficult to live with, even if I do sometimes leave food out on the counter, even if I do sometimes hurt its feelings with pointed sarcastic barbs, you know I love you, robot, don't you? Here's a batch of flowers that I picked up this morning. Aren't they gay? No? I could always return it for something else, yes? Like an angel Hummel? Or a clock in the shape of a hot dog? Just let me know, as the Dollar Mart closes in a few. Beautiful, beautiful, beautiful robot!

HI, EVERYBODY!!!

A Paid Advertisement from
Your Good Friend "Wild Child Tony"

Hey, fellow Bulldogs! How are you?

First of all, welcome back to high school! I do hope your summer was absolutely fantastic and that you had many, many interesting experiences! Mine was pretty good. I stayed right here in this building, just like I have for the past few decades. Wasn't bored, though. Learned how to type! And I finally finished that papier-mâché model of our town that I've been working on forever and ever! If you're interested, it's in the art room, next to the radiator. (Wouldn't touch it for a few days—still a bit moist, wouldn't you know . . .)

Anyway, if it's all right, I'd like to begin with a little "history lesson," if only for the benefit of the hundreds of incoming freshmen. Bear with me if you've heard this before, sophomores, juniors, and seniors! This won't take long, I promise! Here goes:

My name is Wild Child Tony. On June 6, 1984, on prom night, my mother (class of '85) gave birth to a baby boy (me!) in the handicapped stall of the girls' bathroom. I was then abandoned. Sad, right? Not really! I was discovered by an overnight janitor who kindly raised and looked after me, but who soon died, leaving me to fend for myself within this very school. Sad again, right? No!

Actually, yes, it's a little sad, but I can't complain. I really do love it here! I love to roam the hallways during the day, getting into many wonderful adventures, most of which involve you! What I'm saying, fellow Bulldogs, is that I do not ask for your pity!

And yet . . . to see some of your faces in the halls recently, to see the occasional uneasy glances from some of you as I pass by, upsets me greatly. True, I may not smell as nice as most of you. I may not own a "comb," or a "toothbrush," or a freshly laundered pair of socks, or even a bottle of "shampoo." Sure, I've made more than a handful of students over the years gag and, in one infamous case, yes, I did make a home-economics teacher who now lives in a state far away "suffer a near fatal heart attack" with my ferocious body "stench" that smells vaguely like the couch within my lair.

I'll admit it: I may not be "presentable" in the "traditional" sense. And I may not act entirely "normal" when confronted with a "simple" question or a "reasonable" request. I may "loiter" for hours near your lockers, "fondling" or "licking" or "rubbing up against" your "personal items."

Certainly, I'll be the first to confess that I may not be the "easiest" person in the world to live with, especially in light of my tendency to "attack" those teenage "missionaries" who feel it their moral duty to "de-savage" me through their generic offerings of "adult clothing." But who among us here is "perfect"?

Certainly not me. Okay, I might "act out" more than I am able to consciously "control." I may "panic" in certain situations and curl myself into a "ball" so tight that others can only "pity" me. I may have, at one time or another, been threatened with "arrest," and I may have even "barricaded" myself in the ESL classroom by using "extreme force."

And, yes, I may have once threatened the school's security guard with a "musk" that shoots out of a "secret" gland that no other human seems to "possess" and that the school nurse has been unable to "locate." This security guard may have even become permanently "blinded" and may have even gone slightly "insane." Fine.

My point is that we're not so different, you and I! Granted, I do tend to walk around the school in nothing save for a "loincloth" fashioned out of the front and back sections of the newspaper that you're now holding in your hands, our very own Winston Churchill High's weekly *Observer*. And, admittedly, this "loincloth" occasionally will "slip." And, yes, when this happens, I do have a tendency to become a tad "defensive" and I might even "growl" or "hiss" or "snarl," and I might even "scream at the top of my lungs and rear up my red, swollen behind like a baboon in deep heat."

Furthermore, I may "violently" shake my food-encrusted mane of unwashed hair in your faces and "sniff" your necks with my "outrageously large" nostrils and then "stomp my feet as if I'm performing an exotic dance" and then make a "BM" on the ground just before I "charge." I may also scratch. But am I really that bad?

Granted, I may not be a man who is "well liked" or even "tolerated." But I am a man who—because of a recent judgment brought about by a student who shall go unnamed but whose "future" now remains horribly uncertain—feels that he must, according to a Maryland state "law," put the following statement down onto paper.

I hearby promise to never again . . .

Touch, poke, or prod a student's belongings.

Gently stroke Martha Koch's ponytail without her or her boyfriend's permission.

Streak half-naked through a pep assembly without a properly signed or documented slip.

Attempt to steal 23 pounds of tater tots from the school cafeteria, even though this is the sole manner by which I keep from starving.

Audition for any musical, including, but not limited to, *Fiddler on the Roof* and *Man of La Mancha*.

Convince unwitting freshmen that I am the Judge of the School and should henceforth be known as "His Honor."

Publicly and aggressively attend to my festering wounds caused by my errant homemade tattoos.

Sponge-bathe in the photo lab.

Violently refuse a date to the Sadie Hawkins dance, even though no one in particular has asked me.

And I can now promise all of you, my dear comrades, that I, Wild Child Tony, will never again attempt to sell any of you:

Test answers

metallic figurines

ketchup sandwiches

macramé pep banners

handcrafted counterfeit
yearbooks

Polaroid action shots of yours truly

forged hallway passes

forged report cards

forged diplomas

manuscripts of the self-published
My Name is Wild Child Tony

funny money stolen from foreign exchange students

homemade cotton candy

. . . or any other delightful item that I may have constructed or stolen during my downtime, even though this is the sole method by which I keep from going broke.

Friends, neighbors, fellow Bulldogs, I can promise ALL of that and more.

This is my home. Welcome me.

—W.C. Tony, Class of Forever!!!

(Paid for by Wild Child Tony)

Questions? Comments?
Please stop by Hallway B (in the band room)
and ask for Wild Child Tony,
or "the grown man who lives beneath the tympani"

Some Fabrications to Insert into a Personal Diary

Went to the moon today but came back in time for the PBS special on the origin of flight.

•

Invented a new use for the raisin that might just solve the world-hunger issue. Fingers crossed.

•

Ran into George Clinton, the funk and soul singer, at the Sunrise Mart again. He was buying peppermint-flavored toothpaste, a pack of gum, and a NASCAR-themed scratch-off ticket. Nice guy.

Practiced the sitar for six hours on the roof. Mrs. Culyer next door complained, but I refused to stop. A hummingbird landed on my shoulder.

•

Met a giant named Stuart.

•

This morning, I joined a group of young women walking the indoor mall. Chatted in a casual manner about the price of gas, and then, at around ten, when the mall was just opening for customers, I took me a little snooze in front of the Hot Topic.

•

Swam the length of the Mississippi with a little help from a dolphin, and got some interesting looks from the crabbers.

•

Nothing today, diary.

The Rejection of Anne Frank

Dear Ms. Frank:

Thank you for your handwritten memoir submission that found its way to our office and which we Google-translated from the Dutch. Unfortunately, we receive so many unsolicited teenage diaries composed in European attics that it is impossible to publish each one. We are passing on your diary with regrets, but herewith offer some constructive criticism.

First, though we live in a crass age of reality-TV exhibitionism and social-networking narcissism, a memoir from a 15-year-old is a bit much. Until some time has elapsed, it's very difficult to gain perspective on one's trying teenage years. More importantly, do a young girl's problems matter all that much in the grand scheme of things? Consider waiting to take some creative-nonfiction college courses or, at the very least, traveling abroad before tackling this potentially sentimental material.

Open the action up! Readers love to go on a journey—whether it's a divorcee's spiritual quest through India or a journalist's rollicking cross-country road trip to discover the best beef patties. You've written about a young girl confined to an attic for two years. Be honest—which would you rather take to the beach? Exactly: *The United States of Hamburgers*, now available wherever paperbacks are sold.

While we would not suggest you invent any details, if you have any history of drug use (you *are* in Amsterdam!), this is not the time to be shy.

On a similar note, we must now be ever so vigilant when it comes to fact-checking and memoirs. Granted, our knowledge of history is a little shaky, but did a whole country, led by a psychopathic dictator, *really* set out to eradicate an entire religious group? *And* did the dictator really have a ridiculous-looking Charlie Chaplin mustache? *And* did America really not attempt to intervene for more than three years of atrocities? We'll remind you that we're known for *preemptive* strikes. To be honest, the whole thing sounds more like genre fiction or an action movie— which you might want to contemplate adapting this into. Throw in a couple of shower scenes, and it has the makings of a great PG-13 vehicle.

Can your love interest, Peter van Pels, have a secret? It's funny how little you really *know* someone you have a crush on, even when you share the same space for over 700 consecutive days. Have you read our Young Adult series "Signed, Sealed and Discovered?" Check out the third book, *Junior Year According to Jenny Yarrow*, and please tell us you could have predicted that Corey once accidentally killed someone while vacationing in Cancún while driving an electric-powered sports car. *Secrets*.

Fantasy always works, especially with your tween demographic. Come up with something totally original—for instance, is there any ambiguous historical evidence for the presence, in Nazi Germany, of hot teenage vampires?

We're focusing on authors with broad multimedia platforms. While you were up in the attic, did you have strong Wi-Fi access? If so, we hope you Tweeted or, like a lot of disaffected youth, kept a LiveJournal. Maybe you can start a Facebook group—"I Spent My Formative Years in an Attic!" or some such to catch *Good Morning America*'s attention.

You are a very attractive young girl, and you deserve a more professional photo. Also, smile! *Attitude determines altitude.*

Finally, we know it's very postmodern to resist narrative closure, but even if you don't want to tie up every loose string, readers like a satisfying conclusion. Your last entry is dated Aug. 1, and then . . . what, exactly? Do you have a sequel in the works? Again, please see "Signed, Sealed and Discovered."

We encourage you in a few years to submit a project that's more book-club-friendly. In spite of everything, we still believe that you are a really good writer at heart.

Best,
Jessie Kravitz, Associate Editor

Dear Mister Don DeLillo

(A Rhon Penny Letter)

Thank you for taking the time to open this envelope. As you are no doubt aware from having read my last five letters, time, the very whitest of white noises, is of the essence.

A quick reminder: I am a writer named Rhon Penny (silent *h*), and I am no longer married. I am writing to you today (again) with an exciting proposition that is going to be very difficult to decline. But first, a little background about this crazy "game" we call the "literary world."

Have you heard of a writer named James Patterson? Of course you have. He's only the biggest-selling writer in the book business (sorry, not meant as a personal attack), churning out literally two or three best-sellers a year! So, you're thinking, what's his secret? Guess what? *He uses writing partners.* This is where I come into the picture.

Dan, has it always been a dream of yours to have it both ways? To be able to enjoy the advantages of a wonderful social life wherein you can rewatch *What Women Want* for the hundredth time, or hold an impromptu barbecue in the park with your buddies, while also earning the respect of your peers as a top-flight man of letters? This has always been a dream of *mine*. And it's my thinking that if we join forces—preferably *immediately*—we can make this happen.

Being somewhat familiar with your oeuvre (and knowing how to spell "oeuvre"), I realize that you might not be so quick when it comes to creating book ideas—but I'm incredibly fast. How fast? Since I started this letter, I have come up with four solid concepts:

- A "what if" premise: What if the United States had lost World War II, and another country—perhaps Belgium—had somehow won? Would we now have strange accents and eat mussels all the time?

- A more "high-brow" literary idea: A man no longer loves a woman, and vice versa. I think *a lot* can be done with this.

- Something racial: A guy is bitten by a radioactive chameleon, and wakes up to find he can change skin color depending on who's standing next to him.

- If the website "Ask Jeeves" is to be believed, you once wrote a book about Lee Harvey Oswald

and the Kennedy assassination. How about
turning the tables, and writing about a less
violent, but no less interesting, major event?
The Nathan's Hot Dog Eating Contest? It's
topical and interesting. Let's use it.

Another option would be to do something about
Frank Sinatra (you love him, right?). Maybe a story
about a guy who gets kicked out of the rat pack for
telling Sinatra he couldn't go out that night because
he just popped a frozen macaroni and cheese into the
toaster oven. Or something very similar?

Can we now talk author-to-author? I'm sure you
might have a few questions about this specific writing
arrangement, and I'd be happy to answer them all.
For instance, are you worried about how we'll split the
royalties? Or whether your name will go first in the
byline? Or who will take the "lead" on talk shows? Me
on *All Things Considered*, you on *The View*? Let's not
jump the gun, okay? Here's a question for you, though:
Do you have any old ideas sitting around in your
"trunk" that need freshening up? Most writers, as you
no doubt are aware, are constantly working on a few
things at once. This is what's in my trunk:

- A young man discovers a portal into another
  universe . . . and decides to open a much needed
  Baskin-Robbins. (This manuscript ends at page 52.)

- An unauthorized biography of my mother.
  (She literally has no idea.)

- A book entitled *Something Stinky, Something
  Fine*. (So far, I just have the title, which was an
  in-joke I once had with my former boss Teddy

at Kinko's. Sadly, he just died. But I'm sure he
wouldn't mind if I found a new collaborator.)

- A soldier goes to modern-day Afghanistan for some
  reason and realizes he wants to leave, because
  of all the current craziness. What does he need
  all of this madness for in his life? He only wants
  to sleep. (Just getting started on this one.)

For each of these manuscripts, I will give you what I
have so far, along with an incredibly detailed outline—I
have plenty of time, as I'm currently receiving worker's
comp (I was luckier than Teddy). You will do the same
for your half-baked ideas. I'm sorry to be so brusque
with you, but if we are to become literary partners, it's
better that you know my shortcomings from the very
start. (For the record, I can also be sort of cheap.)

For reasons I can't get into, I must immediately
end this correspondence. But I will not sign off without
saying the following:

Mr. DeLillo—Don . . . I am a very sick man. I happen
to suffer from a little disease called optimism. Is it
catching? I hope so.

> Your future partner in the words,
> Rhon Penny

Open Mic Night, 1:15 AM

This is a song I wrote called "I Just Gotta Hit That Dusty Road." I hope you like it. Here we go now:

And I woke up one morning feeling blue,
Truthfully, I didn't know what to do,
So I turned to my wife and said:
"Woman, I gotta hit the road."
I told her: "Woman, I just gotta hit that road."

One of the Lexus's tires blew out just around six,
Isn't this something I could fix?
What would Charlie Patton do?
AAA came right away, sent an entire crew.

Limped into a Motel 6 in Raleigh 'round midnight,
Called the ol' lady, she told me:
"Boy, you ain't coming back, you heard right?"
I said: "Maybe this life ain't for me.
I miss the kids and I miss you—"
And she replied, "Shut the fuck up." (x2)

Spoken: Now what was I supposed to do? Return to my
job as a corporate-tax specialist for a midsize law firm
in northern Virginia? Give up on this lifelong dream of
becoming a singer/songwriter troubadour, a ramblin'
man, laying down the miles, crisscrossing the back roads
of this magnificent nation, carrying nothing except for
my feverish aspirations? Don't think so, thank you very
much! Four, three, two, one . . . and kick it:

Tried to earn some coin by singing my songs,
Audiences didn't take too kindly, but don't get me wrong,
They threw me some change, a nickel here, a dime there,
A dollar once outside a Fuddruckers in Delaware.

Went a little crackers, around the twenty-first of June,
Don't remember much, I was dancing to my own tune.
Ended up in the backyard of my first serious girl,
"Hey, whatya say," I screamed, "let's give it another whirl!"

Spoken: Maybe I should also mention that I was crouched
on her roof and wearing only a fez. And . . . if you saw me
perform last night, please join in . . .

"Hell's happened to you?" she asked, taken aback.
Said I: "Had to follow my dreams! Trying to break out of
*   the pack!"*
"You must be going through a crisis," she cried,
*   slamming the door.*

She then put on some clothes, tho I can't really be sure.

Spoken: She never did return my e-mails, although I have since heard from her blue-collar hubby—he could have been a hell of a lot nicer. And to the rafters now . . .

Sold the Lexus for a can of Pringles and a new guitar,
Got drunk on homemade hooch and followed the stars.
Went on doing my writing, went on doing my singing,
Played for a group of blacks outside Baltimore,
    took a horrendous beating.

Spoken: I would now play a solo on the guitar, but this sling prevents me from doing so. Also, I lost the guitar. Plus, I never learned. Count it down now:

Slept the next few months in an abandoned car,
Woke up each morning next to a whore
    sporting a Z-shaped scar.
Walked across the country, dispensing,
    through my songs, advice,
Like this little ditty about the forty-seven-year-old
    with the nasty case of pubic lice.

Spoken: You might have noticed a bit of foaming in my pants, right? It's the Nix shampoo. Takes a few hours to settle. Where was I? See . . .

Fell into a deep depression,
    where I'd sleep was anyone's guess,
How the hell did I get myself into this goddamn mess?
I'm no blues singer, just a middle-aged man
    with a law degree.
Called my wife one day (collect)
and had her listen to my plea:

"Woman, I think I done made a tremendous mistake,
Just wanted to play the blues,
    but your boy's ready for a break!
All I've ever wished for, really, was to become B.B. King,
Now I'm just your average lawyer
    sufferin' from a strong strain of gangrene.

My woman, she told me: "I just found myself a new man.
Actually that's not true, in all honesty, I don't want to
    stay married to you."
And I cried: "Woman—"
And she replied: "Shut the fuck up." (2x)

Spoken: Can you hear me way in the back? The man
tickling his date? Okay, I'll sing a little louder . . .

If there's a moral to this blues song,
    it goes a little like this . . .
I always yearned to become a blues singer,
hit that dusty road and catch that last train,
See, I had no intention of pissing my life down the
    goddamn metaphorical drain.
Sometimes it's best not to follow your dreams . . .
My last one hundred meals have all involved ice cream.

Spoken: I hope y'all have enjoyed my ode to the
wanderin' life . . . It's been one hell of a ride! I'll be
working through the end of this month, and perhaps
every month, as a bus boy around the corner at The
Bearded Clam, right here in good ol' Morehead City,
North Carolina. If any of you have any spare change,
or maybe a few curly fries, I'd most greatly appreciate
it . . . I sure as heck would! Or a place to stay. Or a
ride back to northern Virginia. I really do miss my

family and my washing machine. It surely has been a pleasure, and I thank y'all very, very much. For the record, I also miss my 27-inch Panasonic flat-screen. God bless.

Arse Poetica

Thanks for having me over and listening to my movie pitches. When my fiction-writing classmates at the Iowa Writers' Workshop heard I was headed to Los Angeles to make it as a screenwriter, they called me a sellout. But if "selling out" implies meeting with the industry's most respected producer of hardcore pornography—well, then, *quand meme*.

Is this your *Adult Video News* award for "Best All-Girl Feature?" I never realized how heavy these things were. And so accurately to scale! Some day, Lord willing.

Sure, if it helps you focus, I don't mind if you pop *Little Latin Lolita* into the ol' DVD. I'm partial to the Kubrick original myself, but I can see where there might be room for character development. If you could just turn down the volume a splash, I'd appreciate it.

My first idea is based on a story that won honorable mention in the 2009 *Omaha Review* debut-fiction contest. I envision shooting it with a Raymond Carver–esque minimalism. My God, can you imagine what that would look like? I actually can't, so I was hoping you or your director of photography would. You don't use a D.P.? But I see it listed on all your films. Double-*what*? Oh boy.

Anyhoo, *Suburban Afternoon* focuses on a stale marriage between a couple in their mid-fifties—maybe early fifties if you want to skew younger. The wife's quotidian routine is interrupted one afternoon by a succession of muscular young refrigerator repairmen, pool boys, and pizza deliverymen all gamely offering her their "services." But here's the twist! By the end, we find out that these young guys were indeed presenting commercial services and nothing more: The fridge really was broken, the pool desperately needed cleaning, and her husband had just ordered an extra-large pie with sausage—some nice metaphorical possibilities with that. And here's the "money shot": an extreme close-up of this woman's face as she has a Joycean epiphany remembering the first time she slept with her husband, when they were young and reckless romantics. We don't see it in a flashback—kind of gimmicky—but it's etched across her features as surely as her crow's-feet.

Come to think of it, that might be less Carver and more Dick Yates. No, he was a writer.

Roxxxanne Bangs? As the female lead? But she's in her late thirties—a little young, right? You mean, she's coming in? Well, I don't see why not. Perhaps she'd be interested in the next pitch? Sure, I can film you while I talk. Now, that's what I call a detached-third-person point of view! Yes, you're in frame.

In *Locker Room Confidential*, the star high-school quarterback has a voice-over—I know that's a cardinal sin in film, but this would be a *retrospective* voice-over about his senior year, so the tension between his present and past selves will create a Barthesian seam of pleasure for the audience. Close, but more like a *mental* seam of pleasure. The quarterback—let's call him Nick, for the Gatsby-like unreliable narrator—has been flirting all year with the head cheerleader. We play against type here; Franny's sexy, of course, but her dialogue is loaded with wry observations reminiscent of the young Virginia Woolf. Virgin*ia*. There you go, like Dick Yates—you're catching on. After the team wins the championship game, Franny finds Nick alone in the locker room. What do you think happens next? Bow-chicka-bow-bow: She reveals she's lost faith in the spiritual world, and he divulges his anxieties about having to live up to the masculine ideals of his horse-wrangler father. Hel-*lo!* Talk about your denial of character expectations!

Absolutely, the more the merrier—it's a free country, and a spacious finished garage. Lisa Lipps *and* Hunter Pierce! Gosh, forgive me if I'm a little starstruck! That's all right, I'll just move back a few feet.

Can you hear me while you're doing that? Super. My last concept is kind of experimental. *Lower Education*. It's a campus satire in the *Lucky Jim* vein about a brilliant but unsung graduate student. Also, he's extremely well-endowed—and, trust me, I'm not talking about his measly graduate stipend! The story is a frank look at his relationship with a beautiful undergraduate whose class he T.A.'s. Uh, teaching assistant. The frisson between them is a literary dance of seduction whereby the undergrad writes a novella ostensibly about migrant laborers in the Depression, but which, to the astute reader, is subliminally packed with unquenched eroticism. And the grad student reciprocates desire through sexually charged line edits—"Beautiful simile," "Elegant verb," "Never split an infinitive, unless you must."

Still with me? So, the revision process rises to a frenzied climax until, thanks to all his hard work, *From My Dusty Hands to Your Chapped Lips* wins the grand prize in the 2009 *Omaha Review* debut-fiction contest, she signs with some hotshot literary agent who just happens to know her aunt, and he realizes that publishing is all about nepotism and not the quality of the writing. And off he heads to La-La Land on a Greyhound with nothing but his wits and a dog-eared copy of *How Hollywood Works, from Top to Bottom*. You're probably asking: Where's the sex? Well, there isn't any! Except for the offscreen sex the coed is probably having with that blond idiot communications major she always hangs out with in Der Rathskeller. That is, it's a porno *not* weighed down by pornographic content! I'm mostly interested in subverting genre here. But if we throw in some subtle allusions to Cleland's

Fanny Hill: Or, Memoirs of a Woman of Pleasure, the audience will definitely get what we're doing. No, not "off"—just "get."

Were those three consecutive shouts of "Yes!" in response to my ideas, or . . . okay, let me just set this camera and boom mic down and leave all four of you alone to mull it over. Make that five—didn't see you down there, Qarizma. How funny! All of this kind of reminds me of an ending to a Flannery O'Connor story! A sprinkle of sad, a dash of redemption, and a healthy dollop of messy!

"O'Connor." You don't have to scream the "O" part. She wrote *A Good Man Is Hard*—never mind.

The Bachelor Party: What You Need To Know

Gentlemen,

I want to thank you all for joining us this Saturday as we celebrate my brother Tom's last day as a free man. I know many of you don't know Tom very well— he's not an easy man *to* know—which is why, in close collaboration with his psychotherapist, nutritionist, life coach, spiritual guide, and second psychotherapist, I've written up the following guidelines.

For the love of God, read them carefully.

We'll kick things off at 11:00 AM sharp. It's probably a bit earlier than you expected, or might care for, but it usually takes a while to coax Tom out of his room. We'll beg through the door for a few hours, sing some happy songs, and loudly pretend he's missing out on all the Cheetos we're enjoying. When he finally lets us in, no more than three of us will be able to occupy the room at any given time. The room is very small, and one of Tom's chief fears is that bandits are always out to surround him. So while a few of us are partying in Tom's room, the rest of us can chill out against the wall in the hallway.

No strippers, fellas. Sorry! Tom's under the impression that pregnancies can—and usually do—occur via lap dances. Over the years, I've tried explaining biological realities to Tom using a variety of books, charts, and anatomically correct hand puppets, but no dice. For the record, Tom's also a bit worried that an impregnated stripper could somehow use a baby as leverage to steal his collection of unused plastic straws.

No alcohol, either, I'm afraid. For reasons Tom has never made entirely clear, fermented things make him sulk. The chemical enhancement for the evening will be Gatorade. The electrolyte boost will usually make Tom see tracers, which is always good for a giggle, until it becomes horrifying.

There *will* be music, though. Tom's learning to play the spoons, but as a beginner he only plays one real spoon against an air spoon. So, that's what I mean by there will be music.

Sorry, gentlemen: No party favors. In other words, no goofy hats, Hawaiian leis, X-rated Mardi Gras beads, ironic pimp canes, feather handcuffs, or blow-up booby balloons. Or whores named Donna. Do you remember what happened at my bachelor party last January? And how it took a few hours to coax Tom out of the Burger King bathroom? Let's avoid that.

Tom's highly allergic to more than a dozen common foaming agents found in shampoos and soaps. I've listed each of them on the back of this brochure, so compare those to your bottles at home. (Tom has indicated that Prell within 10 feet will kill him, outright.) Honestly, it'd be best if you didn't wash your body or your hair within at least 48 hours of the bash, but if you must, consider the homemade rinse (recipe also on back) fashioned out of honey, purified water, and other natural, organic ingredients shipped over from New Zealand. Not cheap. But, I can promise you, worth it.

Avoid prolonged eye contact with Tom. He thinks that people look him directly in the eye because they're peering straight through to his brain, which they covet.

You might not want to ask my brother about the bride, Mary. Even if he does answer, he offers very few details other than "She's a good speller," and "It's hard to tell from a photo, but she seems to be about my height and girth."

Don't say the word "nonpareil" in Tom's presence. Just don't do it.

By 5:30, a few party vans will (hopefully!) be pulling into the driveway in neutral and not in any way beeping or screeching to a halt. Time to party like hell, gentlemen! (We will have approximately five to ten minutes until we reach the parking lot at the Wal-Mart, where all of our cars will be parked, ready to take us home.)

Those are the basics—specifics to come. Generally speaking, if Tom tenses up, licks his lips furiously, or rams his head through the window, just backtrack a tad and change the subject to something he enjoys. We don't know what that is, but, hey, you could get lucky. You had better.

We're gonna have a blast, dudes!

Keith

"Out-of-Office E-Mails" That Might Not Fly with Those in Charge

I will be out of the office until May 23 because I'm taking a "voyage quest" into the woods behind my condominium. I will be bringing with me only a can of beans and an issue of *Swank*. So, obviously, "not reachable" . . .

I will be out of the office until Feb. 17. Nothing serious, just a "crimes against humanity charge" that desperately needs to be addressed before I leave for the Super Bowl in Tampa next week . . .

I will be out of the office until June 1, because two days should be plenty of time to conceive a friggin' child . . .

Annual pilgrimage to John Wayne Gacy's childhood home . . . Relax! Will def. bring back salt-water taffy.

I will be out of the office until August 6th because I'm trying to reunite the cast of "Wings" for my birthday surprise party which is August 4th at my house (1609 S. Hayworth) at 7:00 PM sharp (key next to the garden statues of J.C., Buddah, and Muhammad play-wrestling)

I will be out of the office until November 9th because there just happens to be one very tenacious tapeworm that doesn't seem to want to "exit the premises." Anyone got a match?

I will be out of the office until late next week as my mother-in-law has suddenly become very squeamish about my right to walk around nude in the house that I shall soon inherit from her

Home sick again. Tequilas + dock whores + cops + a lawyer fresh out of correspondence school does not exactly equal "a work mood that's conducive to getting things done." See all you workhorses on Monday. . .

Jimmy Jam Johnson, The Classic-Rock DJ Sufferin' a Nervous Breakdown!

5:45 AM

"That was Boston, 'More Than a Feeling.' Fun fact: they say that Tom Scholz, the creative force behind Boston, took anywhere from five to six months just to record one guitar lick. You want to hear another interesting fact? I hear that goddamn song one more time, I might just do something I'm very much gonna regret. Saw a heavenly light above the house again this morning. Was in the shape of a giant heart. This is Heart, 'Magic Man.'"

6:13 AM

"Kansas, 'Carry On Wayward Son.' Do you know what happened when I rose above all the noise and confusion? More headaches. Met a young woman once who later became my wife. She had a tasty mole above her right nipple. Used to make me do all the right things for all the wrong reasons. Made me lettuce sandwiches with just the thinnest layer of heartbreak. You never tasted heartbreak so tangy. Didn't need mustard or ketchup, that you can believe. Lord almighty, I do still love her. Why did she leave? Did it have to do with the lasers that shoot out of my eyes? Uh oh! My toes are hot. I just lit them on fire. Van Halen. 'Hot for Teacher.' "

6:45 AM

"Okay, okay, we know already! You're a toker, you're a joker. But are you a hero? Need a hero, listeners, a savior of sorts. After the divorce was finalized, I gave myself a little bath in the office's kitchen sink. Washed away my past. Then left accounting and, like a butterfly, molted into Jimmy Jam Johnson, the DJ suffering a nervous breakdown! This ain't shtick, ladies and gentlemen. So now I'm just waiting for a friend. So are the Stones."

6:46 AM

"Wake up, people! Sixty-six degrees, with just the slightest chance of rain. Zip zip! That's the money sound! Be my first caller on the Z-106 hotline and you'll find yourself winning a little trip to my private lair. Speaking of which, found a dead giraffe on my lawn again. I love animals! This is 'House of the Rising Sun.' "

7:23 AM

"Was that just Pink? Or was that Floyd? Whoever it was, tear down that goddamn wall already! Going on around town: It's 'Ladies' Night' at Hammerjacks. 'Popcorn Shrimp Night' at Max's. Spoke to my ex during the last commercial break. Seems that she was none too pleased that I called collect. Who is this elf standing on my palm? I like his can-do spirit. Can't move my arm to save the Ball of Life Fire. Still can't. It's 'Buffalo-Wing Night' at Shooter McGee's. She just bought a house in Tallahassee. It appears that the grad student is moving in. And guess what? Zang-zang-zang! That's the Z-106 party siren! My wife just sent me an invitation. You like weddings? How about white weddings? Billy Idol on the Z-Rock!"

8:14 AM

"Foghat. It's 8:14 on a Monday morning, and I'm taking a 'Slow Ride' to the end of my shift. Or to hell. Or to my townhome off 1-95. My lady and I once made love in a back booth of an Arthur Treacher's. My lady and I once watched a sunset while doing it in an alley behind a Wawa Market. 'We Are the Champions.' I am a puma, all proud and powerful, scanning the Serengeti for a purpose in life. Queen."

8:25 AM

"Hey, Jack. You really wanna forget about Diane? Stay up all night playing Parcheesi alone. Works for me."

8:57 AM

"Alice Cooper. 'No More Mr. Nice Guy.' Last song of the
day, folks. Y'all think I'm a nice guy? You won't after
this story: Gonna show up at my ex's wedding and
punch the grad student in the nose. The spray of blood
will be ferocious. Yours truly gonna be arrested. The
Big Dawg is up next to take you into the noon hour. The
Big Dawg is gonna play that rock-and-roll music nice
and loud. So, until the morn, keep it on the up side but
don't keep it down your pants, because it could bite a
leper. That phrase is trademarked. Just performed a
somersault in my mind! You like gymnastics? I don't.
Hey, what can I say? 'Life's Been Good.' You think so,
Joe? Gotta disagree. Take it away, bro . . . "

Krazy Kris!

January 1

Me: "Listen, can't we talk about this some other time?"

Jen: "Some other time when? Our finances are a disaster! If we don't take care of this situation now, we're going to have to take out a second mortgage. So when do you plan—"

Krazy Kris: "Did someone say mortgage? That reminds me of a joke. What did the man say to the—"

Jen: "Who in the hell is this?"

Me: "This is Krazy Kris! I hired him to provide comic relief! You know, for our relationship! For our lives!"

Jen: "Where did he come from?"

Me: "A special agency. For couples who are a little down. Anyway, look! He's taking off his shirt! He's popping his ample stomach in and out! Isn't this fantastic? Honey? Yes?"

Jen: "How is he supporting himself? What exactly are you paying him?"

Me: "Our 401(k). Relax, it's worth it."

Jen: "Now he's performing somersaults on our living room floor."

Me: "This guy can do anything! Isn't he amazing?"

March 3

Jen: "I really don't know what to do about my mother. We should talk about assisted care versus independent care—"

Krazy Kris: "Look at me, everybody! I'm making balloon animals!"

Jen: "For the love of . . . he has to make an appearance

every time we have a fight? How does he even know
when to come over?"

Me: "I have him paged."

Jen: "He's now playing a tuba and marching in place . . .
I can't hear myself think!"

Me: "Louder! Louder!"

April 6

Jen: "Are you aware that Krazy Kris is standing at the
edge of our bed?"

Me: "I figured we needed to lighten things up a bit in
the bedroom. Mind?"

Jen: "What's that standing next to him?"

Me: "What does it look like? It's a miniature donkey!
Krazy Kris rented it for the night. Isn't she adorable!"

Jen: "We haven't made love in months!"

Me: "It's the perfect remedy to take our minds off our
problems! Kris, make the donkey bray! Do it!"

May 4

Jen: "We really should be talking about assisted care
versus independent care—"

Me: "Sure, sure."

Krazy Kris: "Hey, everybody! Take a look at me! I'm juggling the wedding china!"

July 5

Krazy Kris: "Anyone up for some spin-art fun? Hey, where's your wife?"

Me: "At her brother's in Tampa—she just moved out."

Krazy Kris: "That's terrible. I'm sorry."

Me: "It had absolutely nothing to do with you. Entertain me, Krazy . . . I need it now more than ever."

Krazy Kris: "Doin' the limbo! Grab on tight, folks! We're goin' for a ride!"

August 13

Krazy Kris: "Seen the TV remote?"

Me: "Aren't you going to amuse me?"

Krazy Kris: "How much can I amuse you already? Four hours isn't enough?"

Me: "When you first got here, you'd amuse me all day. How about a handspring?"

Krazy Kris: "Actually, my head is killing me. Maybe later?"

Yesterday

Krazy Kris: "I think my troubles first started in college. Women could never relate to me as anything more than a friend. Always the funny guy, you know?"

Me: "God, you're a bore. What's the matter with you lately?"

Krazy Kris: "I guess even clowns have their off months, right? So sue me. Life ain't all about the gags. Pass my reading glasses."

Today

Krazy Kris: "Seen the heating pad? My back is on fire. Oh, I'm in such a mood!"

Me: "I think we need to talk, Krazy Kris."

Krazy Kris: "About what? And by the way, my real name's Christopher."

Me: "I miss the juggling, the spontaneity, the animal tricks. It's not like it used to be."

Krazy Kris: "Welcome to life, big man."

Me: "All I'm saying is that we need to have a little chat."

Krazy Kris: "Ha! Give me a break! Who are you, my father? Here we go again! Pick, pick, pick! Like a goddamn crow!"

Me: "Well, I *am* paying your rent! And for your food! So, yes, maybe I am your father!"

Krazy Kris: "Shut up!"

Me: "Excuse me? Who are you to talk to me like that? Who—"

Mr. Pickles: "Put your hands in the air! Put your hands in the air like you just don't care!"

Krazy Kris: "Who in the hell is this? And why is he wearing a gigantic rainbow wig and playing the ukulele?"

Mr. Pickles: "They call me Mr. Pickles! C'mon, everybody! It's time to dance! Dance! Dance your problems away!"

FW: Loved The Following Jokes
And Thought
You'd Love Them As Well!!!

(Pass Them On)

1.

Two women are playing golf. The first tees off and
watches in horror as her ball heads directly at a
foursome of men playing the next hole.

Indeed, the ball hits one of the men, and he immediately
clasps his hands together at his crotch, falls to the
ground, and proceeds to roll around in agony.
The woman rushes over to the man and begins to
apologize. She says: "Please allow me to help. I'm a

physical therapist, and I know that I could relieve your pain if you'd allow."

"No, I'll be all right . . . I'll be fine in a few minutes," he replies as he remains in the fetal position, still clasping his crotch. But she persists, and he finally allows her to help. She unzips his pants, puts her hands inside, and begins to massage him. She then asks: "How does this feel?"

To which he rejoins: "It feels great, but my thumb still hurts like hell!"

After a short pause, during which nothing is said, there is this exchange:

"You think you're so funny?" jibes the lady, now crying. "I spent many years training to become a physical therapist. My husband has a terrible heart condition, and could die at any time. We're in debt for thousands. The only reason I'm playing golf this morning is to take my mind off all my problems. And I need you and your stupid jokes? I don't think so. You're no comedian!"

The man, too, begins to cry. Wiping his eyes with his sleeve, he cracks: "I'm new at playing practical jokes, and I'm slightly drunk. This is not how I usually act! I promise you that I won't do it again! Okay?"

"Okay," quips the lady, still crying, but not as hard. "All right then, okay."

2.

One day, while on vacation in the big city, two rednecks, Bubba and Daryl, leave their hotel to have dinner. Tired and hungry, they decide to stop in at a kosher deli.

After having a seat, they ask the waitress what the house specialty is. She replies that it's matzo-ball soup.

A few minutes later, the waitress brings the bowls of soup to Bubba and Daryl. They've never seen anything quite like this, but, being hungry, they quickly eat the soup.

After they finish, the waitress arrives.

"How did you like your soup?" she asks.

To which Bubba zings: "Mmm-mmm, that was good! But tell me . . . do you Jewish folks eat other parts of the matzo, or just the balls?"

There is no laughter, just silence, broken only by the sound of the waitress grinding her dentures. Are they making fun of me? she thinks. Or are they just being cute? She's not quite sure.

"Are you making fun of me?" asks the waitress.

"Listen," says Bubba, "we're only making fun of ourselves. Let's face it, we look just like two hicks, so we enjoy playing up the stereotype. No big deal. Just a joke. We actually love matzo ball soup!"

The waitress, not believing him, grabs the first item that she can find, a wooden broom handle, and begins to swing wildly. She sets upon the two with a vengeance, all the while trying not to disturb the dinner party taking place upstairs.

She hates being mocked more than anything.

3.

A boy is walking down the street when he notices his grandpa sitting in his rocking chair on the front porch, wearing nothing from the waist down.

"Grandpa, what are you doing?" the boy asks.

The old man looks off in the distance and does not answer.

"Grandpa, what are you doing sitting out here with nothing on below the waist?" the boy inquires.

Without missing a beat, the old man retorts: "Well, last week I sat out here with no shirt on, and I got a stiff neck. So, this is your grandma's idea!"

The air is still, and in the distance, a car horn can be heard.

The boy, not saying anything, just stares at his grandfather's aged, sickeningly white penis. After a few moments, the boy takes a bite out of his peanut-butter sandwich, waves good-bye, and leaves for his friend Jeffrey's house.

Things You *Must* Do Before You Grow Too Old

Drink from big-boy cup

•

Emerge nude, from a large, hollow cake, into an empty, cavernous banquet hall

•

Have sexual relations while listening to "Crazy Train"

•

Dismount the mechanical bull you've been riding for 28 years

End a business transaction without the words
"No condom, no yum-yum"

•

Solo on your steel drums in public

•

Patiently explain to your elderly uncle what
genderfucking is all about

•

Be the first person in your family to pass a
Breathalyzer test knee-deep in a swamp

•

Get trampled by hogs

•

Give a PowerPoint presentation without being
steadied by angel dust

•

Mail *The Golden Child* back to Netflix

•

Walk around Disney World clutching a samurai sword

•

Cheer up a sick child by wearing a clown nose fashioned
from a red enema ball

•

Feel the rush of breaking your back in a
trampoline accident

•

Dance like nobody's watching or laughing or
throwing garbage at you

Tug frantically at emergency chute

•

Become a member of Greyhound Bus Line's infamous "36-Inch-High Club"

•

Spend a crisp fall day buying panties from a Japanese vending machine

•

Be the first in the neighborhood to flee from an encroaching minority group

•

Volunteer to be the first citizen in space with a severe inner-ear problem

•

Ask for a raise. And then a job.

•

Blast the shit out of House of Pain's "Jump Around"

•

Design the perfect cape

•

Tell your in-laws how much you love them and need them to invest in your frozen-yogurt business

•

Visit Martha's Vineyard and talk to Carly Simon about stuff

•

Stow away behind the amps on a Sammy Hagar Cabo Wabo Around-The-World Cruise

Visit Walden Pond and laconically
masturbate in a canoe

•

Forgive Bono

•

Really get your delts looking super-tight

•

Let someone besides your bookie cut your hair

•

Join the Klan—but only attend the
barbecues and toy drives

•

Just once, really jam on the funk

THE ZAPRUDER FILM:
THE NOVELIZATION

The Photo Captions

#1. Beverly Oliver (the babushka lady) and Abraham Zapruder discuss their burgeoning relationship's inevitable growing pains.

#2. Jacqueline Kennedy and J. Edgar Hoover stand on the grassy knoll: "Mr. Hoover, I will do everything in my power to prevent your wrecking ball from tearing down the Children's Community Center & Book Depository!"

#3. Carlos Marcello and Fidel Castro plan the bank heists.

#4. Meanwhile, on the outskirts of Las Vegas, our exhausted bachelors, John and Bobby Kennedy, are met with a most festive welcome!

#5. Lee Harvey Oswald and his arch-nemesis, Vaughn Meader, prepare for the championship karate fight.

#6. The top-secret legal brief!

#7. The car chase between Richard Nixon and Governor Connally winds through the crowded and hilly streets of San Francisco.

#8. Mr. Nixon—standing next to his stalled green pickup truck—attempts to flag down a van full of attractive stewardesses.

#9. "Dick, spread that tanning oil on my back *just* right!"

#10. Bar fight at Ruby's Place, where Nixon nurses a black eye . . . and new friend J. Edgar Hoover can only laugh!

#11. The computer screen.

#12. After making love to Beverly by the Union Terminal Tower, Abraham pops the question.

#13. Jackie in the midst of her final argument before the Supreme Court. "In conclusion, your honor, you must not allow the Children's Community Center to be torn down! You can't! And you *must* not!"

#14. From one bank heist to the next, Carlos and Fidel make their presence felt!

#15. Baboo, the talking orangutan, makes everyone laugh!

#16. John and Bobby wake up with hangovers . . .

#17. . . . and can't find their wallets!

#18. The hookers have 'em! Hugs all around!

#19. "I do!" says Beverly. "Yes, I *will* marry you, Abraham Zapruder!"

#20. Baboo gives a cop the finger, and sticks out his tongue! Now he blows a raspberry!

#21. Round 7 . . . Oswald delivers a karate chop to Vaughn's torso. How can Vaughn stand the punishment? But what's this? Is the possum act working?

#22. The car chase wends its way back to Texas, as Nixon and Connally step on it!

#23. The pinewood outdoor accent by Pottery Barn.

#24. "And so, in light of the brilliant final summation that we have just heard, the Supreme Court rules in favor of Jackie. The Children's Community Center must not be torn down! It shall stand!"

#25. A smiling J. Edgar Hoover finds it difficult to remain steamed! A good sport . . . to the end.

#26. The hot-air balloon.

#27. Beverly and Abraham prepare for their elaborate wedding in the grand foyer of the Book Depository.

#28. Fidel and Carlos count their blessings . . . and their earnings. And, feeling generous, they exclaim: "Your wedding is on *us*, Abraham Zapruder! Think nothing of it!"

#29. Perfection . . . but where are Bobby and Jack?

#30. Arrival . . . in the nick of time!

#31. Nixon and Governor Connally also show up for the laughs . . .

#32. . . . by crashing through the reception! With the stewardesses and kindly hookers!

#33. Uh-oh! Pie fight . . .

#34. "Look out everybody! John Kennedy is about to get hit with a coconut-cream! Right on the nose! Nice shot, Baboo!"

#35. Framed wedding photo: John, Bobby, J. Edgar, Beverly, Jackie, Abraham, Carlos, Fidel, and the rest of the gang. Friends forever . . .

#36. "And the new karate champion is . . . Vaughn!"

#37. "You won this time, Vaughn, but I *will* be back."

#38. Freeze-frame.

#39. Sunset.

#40. EMF's "Unbelievable." Credits.

#41. Bloopers!

#42. OUCH! That smarts!

#43. Kennedy mispronounces "Ouch!"

#44. Oswald gets hit, too . . . right in the testicles!

#45. Film and soundtrack available on iTunes.

Game-Show Catchphrases That Never Quite Caught On

"So . . . do you want to lick it, pump it, or tickle it?"

•

Studio audience (in unison): "TIME! TO! FIND! THE!
CASHEW!!!"

•

"Pull the plug, or let your mother lie in a vegetative
state for another few years?"

•

"I'm-a gonna kiss you. Happy? Scared?"

"For one hundred more dollars or one thousand
more amps of current, which president was known for
his (inaudible) and often (inaudible) habits?
(Very clearly) Well?"

•

"Congratulations! You must now make a decision as to
whether or not one of your twins will be sat upon by
that fat man in silhouette eating a glazed donut behind
the lacy curtains."

•

"A job that you don't like all that much, or hanging
around at home for the rest of your life in paper
slippers, watching reruns of this very show?"

•

"Mind if I touch your 'pink'?"

•

"Put the cup to your lips and, for a million dollars and
the chance to be revived, GUESS YOUR POISON!"

•

"Would you like to buy a vowel? You wouldn't? Then how
about a prosthetic nose?"

•

"It's time for this young contestant to decide if he wants
to be ugly or rich! Release the rabid bonobos!"

•

"Time is running out. What's your final answer
regarding this large, red sore on my right heel?"

•

"Studio audience, help me out! There's only one way to
win on this game show, and that's to . . .
CRAP! YOUR! PANTS!"

My Parents, Enid and Sal, Used to Be Famous Porn Stars

ENID: "Yes? May I help you? Why are you knocking on my front door?"

CHUCK: "Ma'am, I work as a roof repairman. I just turned nineteen, and I'm in terrific shape. It's really hot out here, and I am very thirsty. I'm also quite hungry. My appetites are insatiable."

ENID: "A roof repairman, huh? Do you have any references?"

CHUCK: "No, but I am very lonely."

ENID: "No references!"

CHUCK: "No, ma'am."

ENID: "Can you fix gutters?"

CHUCK: "I can fix *anything.*"

ENID: "Hmmmm, that's a good skill. What are your rates?"

CHUCK: "Ma'am, if you'd just let me into the house, I think you'd be plenty pleased . . . "

ENID: "I wouldn't be so sure of that. Bad experiences with handymen in the past. Sloppy work."

CHUCK: "Nothing sloppy about me. Here, let me take off my shirt. And my pants."

ENID: "You're just wasting my time. Send me your estimate. And I'll think about it. Maybe in the fall."

CHUCK: "But . . ."

SAL: (from family room) "Close the goddamn door already! The blasted air-conditioning!"

—from *Let's Face It, The Roof Didn't Need Fixing Anyway*, 1999

NURSE CHERRY: "So what seems to be the problem today? Anything I can help you with?"

SAL: "Just an annual checkup."

NURSE CHERRY: "The doctor's running a little late this morning. In the meantime, I'd like to give you my own special exam. I'm a very *talented* nurse."

SAL: "No, I'd rather wait for the doctor."

NURSE CHERRY: "Are you *sure*?"

SAL: "Yes."

NURSE CHERRY (seductively): "Are you *positive*?"

(long pause)

NURSE CHERRY (less seductively): "I'll go get the doctor."

—from *Office Like a Damn Freezer!*, 2000

PORSHA: "I can't believe that we are the only ones left in the entire library!"

SAL: "Sorry, I was looking for—my god, you're not wearing pants! Or shoes!"

PORSHA: "I'm a dirty, dirty librarian!"

SAL: "I can see that! Your feet are filthy. Do you always walk around barefoot in public?"

PORSHA: "Not always. Sometimes I wear high heels. Would you like to see them? Here, let me just—"

SAL (a little sadly): "So, what you're telling me is that, in essence, I'm paying taxes so that you may frolic about in the buff, with high heels?"

PORSHA: "No, I . . ."

SAL (more upbeat): "No need to apologize. But this is what I want you to do: I want you to put on a sensible pair of slacks. When you're done, I'd like the June issue of *Consumer Reports*. With the dishwashers. No rush, honey, take your time."

—from *Place Like a Damn Sauna*, 2001

SAL: "Let me just put on my glasses . . . can't quite figure out how this works . . . where's the 'on' button? . . . if my son were here, he'd know . . . electronics not really my specialty . . . instructions would really help . . . still can't find the 'on' button . . ."

—from *At the Orgy*, 2003

ENID: "Now let's see . . . what do I need here . . . "

BO: "Hello there!"

ENID: "Hello."

BO: "I see that you're shopping for nuts."

ENID: "I always shop for nuts."

BO: "Do you like nuts?"

ENID: "Yes."

BO: "How about buns?"

ENID: "Sure, nuts and buns."

BO: "Would you like to see my nuts and buns?"

ENID: "No, thank you, I have my own nuts and buns."

BO: "I think you'll like mine better . . . a whole lot better."

ENID: "Do you work here in the grocery?"

BO: "Yes, my name is Bo. And I am in charge of the nuts and buns."

ENID: "Like I said, Bo, I have my own nuts and buns. But I am very curious about something: I noticed that the whole-grain hamburger rolls were listed on sale in the newspaper, but they're still regular price on the shelves. The difference is sixty-five cents, which may not be a lot for you, but it is for me. Here, come along and I'll show you. Perhaps we can solve this problem together."

BO: "You don't want to see my nuts?"

ENID: "No, thank you. But I simply adore your bedazzled leather shorts! Did you fashion them yourself, Bo?"

—from *Double-Coupon Day*, 2004

SAL: "Blasted map!"

ENID: "Pull over and ask that hitchhiker for directions."

SAL: "Where?"

ENID: "Over there. Can't you see her? The young woman in the bikini? She's holding a large cardboard sign that reads: LOOKING FOR A 3-WAY!"

SAL: "What the hell does that mean?"

ENID: "It's probably the slang."

SAL: "Whatever it means, she probably has no idea where Route 116 is. Forget it. Why ask for trouble?"

—from *I Mean, Really, Why Ask for Trouble?*, 2009

Everyday Tantric Positions!

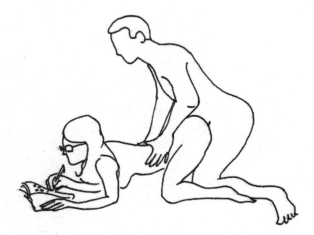

The "Multi-Tasking While Filling Out a Sudoku Puzzle"

The "I Need to Wear These Driving Gloves
Because of My Eczema"

The "I Can't Believe We Just Met at the Hospital Chapel"

The "How Do You Like My Giant Foam Cowboy Hat?"

**The "Please Don't Eat the Chili Dog on Our
New Tempur-Pedic Mattress"**

The "Careful, Please, the Home Vasectomy Hasn't Healed Yet"

The "Hurry, I'm Due Back at the Piercing Pagoda"

The "Obvious Miscommunication of Fantasy Themes"

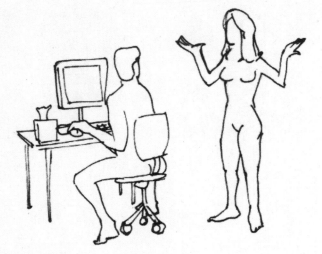

The "Caught Looking at Mexican-Midget Porn"

The "I Hate to Complain, But Your Award-Winning
Horned Lizard Is Licking My Toes"

Hey Babe

Hey Babe:

I've been thinking about what you said re: my "controlling" ways. I will continue to reflect on your remarks, and we'll talk more upon my return from this business trip. Can't wait to see you!!!

Love, Me

XXX OOO SSS YYY NNN BBB PPP TTT
FFF QQQ DDD GGG WWW HHH MMM VVV
RRR JJJ LLL

P.S.—Sigh . . . I can almost hear you now from where I sit! Are they that difficult to remember? Would you like a quick refresher? Okay, then, a quick refresher . . .

X = a kiss

O = a hug

S = a saucy lick

Y = a solid handshake, very businesslike. Not too hard, but not too soft. Let's get it right.

N = nude calisthenics, preferably before a large mirror, and with appropriate lighting.

B = an exciting, powerful high five, the kind old high-school buddies might share at a sports bar when the team they've been rooting for their whole lives scores a winning touchdown, and they slap palms knowing that no matter how many ways life might prove terrifying and unknowable, moments like this are exactly as they should be.

P = staying in on a Friday night to play Scrabble and drink red wine. Even though you prefer white, we'll both drink red.

T = remember that day at the park? That day when we walked hand in hand alongside the reflecting pool and then strolled, ever so casually, over to the cocker spaniel with the very bad breath and that vague, faraway stare that reminded me of the rabid dog I once saw beneath the arts-and-crafts cabin at summer camp? I'm recalling that memory as I write this. You should be, too.

F = a strangely stilted, almost lackadaisical embrace, with just the slightest hint of the most rakish of winks. (This one is *enormously* complicated. Please refer to the diagram hanging on the fridge.)

Q = a delicious ear nibble, making sure not to draw blood this time. Sorry about the last time! Can't believe I swallowed that gold earring.

D = a drive over to the Nadlers for dinner. They've been wanting to have us over for months now. So what if they don't expect our arrival? They adore surprises!

G = you wander into a bank robbery gone wrong and the gunman grabs you because he knows that the police would never let someone so attractive be killed. The police give the gunman a jet to Bermuda, and he escapes thinking he's in the clear. Meanwhile, he doesn't know that I've stowed away in the baggage compartment. I sneak into the cockpit and murder the gunman using martial arts that I've somehow mastered. It's only then that I deal with the logistics of

trying to land the plane and explaining to my boss why
I missed work.

W = both of us in bed, side by side, watching *America's
Got Moxie* with our tops off. I'm holding the clicker. You're
nursing a glass of flavored seltzer, and trying to remember
if you did the Word Scramble in Sunday's newspaper.

H = a sensuous massage with exotic scents and fancy
oils. If we can find no fancy oils, then let's just use olive
oil. Truthfully, it's a hell of a lot cheaper. Put that on the
grocery list, please.

M = I'm late for our dinner date. You're waiting for me
at the bar, and you have your back turned when I enter.
I stand behind you and say, joking, "Buy you a drink?"
You turn to say that you're meeting someone, but then
you discover it's me and, instead of laughing, you say
only, "Scotch. Neat." I order the drinks, and ask you
your name.

V = you give me a fake one: "Marie." And I respond in
kind with: "Leonid." Neither of us laughs. Neither of
us backs out of the game we're playing, two longtime
lovers pretending to be strangers at a bar, strangers
who wonder where things might lead, even though the
minute they laid eyes on each other they knew exactly
what they wanted.

R = at dinner's end you say "Follow me," and I drive behind you as you lead us, not home, but to a motel. You take me into that anonymous room, and we worry aloud about the possibility of bedbugs. You take me with a passion that hasn't been possible since we were in our early twenties. When we're finally finished, we wash our hands thoroughly. We dress quickly and race home to relieve the babysitter. We might want to call first, so she doesn't get nervous.

J = a linking together of our arms, a counter-clockwise gambol, do-si-do and away we go, a change of direction on the second lap . . . this time to the accompaniment of actual music, and not with me blowing trumpet noises through my tightly clenched fist . . . work with me here, c'mon, I can't do this alone . . .

L = all of the above performed incredibly quickly, one after the other, and then—oh, what the hell—one more time in reverse order for good luck.

That wasn't so hard, was it? Sweetheart, I just cannot wait to see you! But do not panic! As with yesterday's batch, you'll get the hang of 'em with a little practice, right? There we go, honey, get crackin' . . . .

When Making Love to Me: What Every Woman Needs to Know

A Cheat Sheet

#1. First of all, welcome. Thank you for coming over. I'd appreciate it if you did not turn off the metronome, it's there for a purpose. Same with the strobe lights.

#2. See?

#3. Feel free to role-play any scene from any movie— I'm quite partial to disaster movies, but I have a very open mind.

#4. Warning: If I faint or lose consciousness, do not panic. If and *when* I regain consciousness, please resume exactly where we left off, or I may have to start over from the very beginning.

#5. Be tender. While I have read literally thousands of instruction manuals, sex has never been my "strong point."

#6. If I begin to laugh uncontrollably, it isn't you. Chances are extremely good that I'm just imagining what my best friend Kurt's reaction will be when I tell him about all this.

#7. Do not take offense if I jot down notes and diagrams for future reference. Furthermore, do not take offense if I refer to said notes.

#8. If you see a man peeking through a window, that's just Kurt.

#9. Love me for who I am and not for what I just did to your armpit.

#10. All eyes on me, *always*.

#11. Yoo-hoo! Over here!

#12. Be respectful of my needs, particularly my need to roll into a ferociously tight ball whenever feeling bored or antsy.

#13. Excuse my impulses: If I burst into wild and ecstatic applause, I have done well and I know it.

#14. If I pull my right leg across my body and pretend to play the air guitar to Jimmy Buffett's "Cheeseburger in Paradise," you will know that I have just done *unusually* well.

#15. Do not point or stare at my very large birthmark. You're shrugging. Thisaway, Sherlock . . . the question mark on the tip of my penis, *there* you go . . .

#16. Important: If you notice a musky, almost overpowering odor, it's not the feral cats.

#17. Nor is it the raccoons.

#18. Nor is it my feet. Actually, it is my feet.

#19. Another thing: If you see me aggressively rolling my eyes, and jutting out my jaw, and making bizarre and extremely loud clicking noises with my tongue, do not become concerned—I'm merely practicing my "game face."

#20. Honor my creative spirit! The life-size replicas of all my ex-girlfriends that you see standing throughout this bedroom are, indeed, for sale. Yes, they are "hand-made" and I do accept cash.

#21. Tickle me until I giggle, but I *beg* of you to know when to stop.

#22. My bad.

#23. Just out of curiosity: Have you ever taken a champagne bath with a lover? Aren't they romantic? Would wine spritzer do?

#24. Ah, yes, one minor issue: Please be extra patient with my inability to bring females to anything close to what the experts might call "climax," "release," or "positive experience."

#25. Do you like my leather sex harness? Isn't it terrific? I bought it for this very special occasion! Go ahead and test it out, although I do request that you try to be super-duper careful—I'm still making payments.

#26. For your sake, that isn't something I'd touch.

#27. And neither is that.

#28. Would *definitely* not touch that.

#29. My bad again.

#30. By the way, I would love to one day turn what happened between us into a stage production, and perform it across the country. I only ask that I be allowed to use your real name.

#31. But more than anything, I want you to have a grand time! Take what you have just learned, and go forth into the world. I thank you for your patience—

#32. Hang on a sec, that's my cell phone. Two nickels to one it's my dermatologist calling with the test results.

#33. Actually, I think it's my identical twin in California! He has a "sixth sense" when things have just gone awry. You know your way out, right?

#34. If not, Kurt will show you. I thank you for your patience, and I wish you the best of luck with any and all future endeavors.

#35. Oh, geez, I almost forgot! This cheat sheet that you now hold in your hands, the one written in Magic Marker on a Hamburger Hamlet menu? The one that you're not accepting for some reason? It's yours to keep. Please ignore the grease and other assorted stains, okay? And with that, I shall now bid you a heartfelt, and deeply felt, adieu. Keep in touch?

Icebreakers to Avoid

"You're not going to believe how many pig anuses
the average hot dog contains."

•

"Quick: Name your top-five favorite Blues Traveler tunes."

•

"Who do I have to fuck at this party to find out
where to take a shit?"

•

"Is it hot in here, or is my body just completely
covered in petroleum jelly?"

"Let's talk about knives."

•

"Isn't this place fabulous? Wouldn't you
just love to die here?"

•

"I can see you're not one of those 'shallow' people
who's super-concerned about appearance."

•

"Sit back, relax, and allow me to explain
the importance of composting."

•

"It's amazing how many people have preconceived
opinions about snuff films."

•

"Were those earrings given to you by a pimp
because you're his favorite baby doll?"

•

"Tell me honestly: Do I look like a rapist to you?"

•

"I don't really see why we need art."

•

"These look like lice, right? Apparently, they're
just chiggers."

•

"What's your dream toothpaste?"

•

"I just found these Sharpies—let's circle
each other's flaws."

"I know what you're thinking, and yes, the picture on my profile was taken before the accident."

•

"Lemme guess. Korean?"

•

"Anybody ever tell you that you look like a young Rocky Dennis from the movie *Mask*?"

•

"Apropos of nothing, I'm going to call you 'Peanut Butter Guy.'"

•

"Do you know the host well, or are you just blackmailing him with photos of his daughter fellating her driving instructor, like I am?"

•

"I think you and I should put on Tron suits and pop a handful of these pink pills."

•

"This party reminds me of 9/11."

•

"You seem like someone who wants to see genuine autopsy photos—am I right, or am I right?"

•

"So I'm like, '*I'll* show you who's afraid to stare directly at the sun!'"

•

"What's your all-time-favorite coupon?"

"You know who I hate? All those poseurs who claim to
be Wiccan without understanding the first thing about
the Three-Fold Law of Return."

•

"Do my palms smell weird?"

•

"The Muppets are bullshit, and let me tell you why."

•

"I really think M. Night Shyamalan is an auteur
in the traditional sense."

•

"May I propose a toast? To the innocent people
who were horribly tortured and executed
this morning in Darfur. *Salud!*"

•

"I wouldn't call them actual voices. More like
hyenas scratching at the walls of my brain."

•

[*APPLYING HAND SANITIZER*] "Nothing personal."

•

"When was the last time you stared into the
headlights of an oncoming car and thought,
Is today the day I grow a pair?"

•

"Everything Smurfy over here?"

•

"They're night-vision goggles, and no,
I won't be removing them."

Dear Mister Salman Rushdie

(A Rhon Penny Letter)

I am a writer named Rhon Penny (silent *h*), and I am
no longer married. I am writing to you today because
I seek advice on how best to deal with a large group of
people trying to kill me.

That is not to say a large group of people want to kill
me at present, but it is my hope that—with your kind
help—I can entice a large group of people to want to kill
me in the near future. You see, as far as I can discern,
the reason I have not yet enjoyed financial or critical

success is not a lack of writing talent. Rather, I have yet to stumble upon a really solid gimmick, such as the fatwa you were lucky enough to be associated with for more than two decades! (Has it really been over two decades? Isn't it funny how quickly time passes?)

Just for the record, here are some other potential gimmicks I have considered:

- Gaining weight like Robert De Niro did in *Raging Bull* (if I'm not mistaken, I don't think an author has *ever* done this)

- Making a book somehow smell like freshly baked cookies (still working on the logistics)

- Putting a mirror on the cover

- Creating a flattering author's photo that will make me appear very handsome, perhaps one of me atop a large, rented black elephant, with my hair combed (for once!), a pipe in my mouth, and holding a Komodo dragon (Hemingway used to do this)

Did I tell you, in my last few letters, about my mother? She's a longtime subscriber to *Writer's Digest* magazine, and knows a thing or two about this bizarro world that we call "the lit game." She has a funny saying: If you want to write, you have to hate. In other words, you need a fire in your belly, which I very much have. I am very angry, and I am also on worker's comp. (I was luckier than my former boss at Kinko's, Teddy, and—except for this shriveled arm—remain blessedly unscathed by the explosion.)

So, after much consideration, and after thinking about this subject over Snackwell's Creme Sandwiches with my mother, currently limited in her activities due to an as-yet-undiagnosed scalp condition, I've decided that the following groups upset me the most. These people must be challenged in print, and *immediately*:

- *Dentists.* Isn't it about time someone called them out for their hypocrisy and moral ambiguity? Everyone despises these so-called doctors! There's a built-in audience for this one.

- *Women.* America is literally swarming with them. And, yes, I am well aware that an anti-women book runs the risk of coming off as "sexist," at least within the "lamestream" media, but I just think they are primed for a good skewering. I also don't find them threatening, because they tend to be weak.

- *Cows.* I truly hate these animals. I am now writing a screenplay called *Sacred Cows*, which I'd be happy to send your way. Imagine if the movie *Babe* met the movie *Precious: Based on the Novel "Push" by Sapphire*, and they adopted the movie *Hoosiers*, and then raised them together in the same ranch-style home. It's exactly like that, but with more basketball.

- *Dog trainers.* I can't stand these people, for very, very personal reasons. But the more I think about it, the less happy I am with this idea. I would prefer groups who have really solid media connections, such as meteorologists, whom I also despise.

Okay, now on to more practical matters. Salman, where in the world should I secrete myself away so that people can't find and kill me? If you could kindly pass along the location of where you hid all those years, that would be amazing. However, if you prefer that I pick my own secret hiding place for enjoying my own fatwa, I could certainly use some assistance in narrowing down the following list:

- A spider hole I built myself in my backyard.

- The crawl space above my ex-wife and her new husband Stew's newly refurbished living room. They have a flat-screen, which should help pass the time nicely.

- Room 54 at the Hampton Inn in Paramus, New Jersey. (I did some online research, and they offer a free continental breakfast.)

- I could also just keep moving from one Chipotle franchise to the next until the fatwa is lifted . . . or I tire of burritos.

- Your house (if you can guarantee a working humidifier and pay for my shingles medication).

Salman, I hear the opening jingle to *Wheel of Fortune*, and so, like the regal fish you yourself were named after, I must return to whence I was born (mother's TV room). But before I scoot, I would be forever in your debt if you would forward me the contact info for your ex-wife Miss Padma Lakshmi. She is very pretty and I feel like she might benefit from getting to know me better. This should also prove that I am not "anti-women."

I look forward to your response. Just so you know, you are free to keep the enclosed WILL WRITE FOR CHOCOLATE baseball cap. I'm assuming that now that your fatwa is finally over, you're more than a little eager to strut around like a big ol' fancy, half-British peacock! Right? There's a whole world out there for you, Sal. Let it be *my* time to hide now . . .

Yours in the words,
Rhon Penny

Shaft in the Suburbs

Groove Time in Potomac, Maryland

Shaft is up early this morning, with a headache roaring through his head like a leaf blower at full throttle. Goddamn leaf blowers—like they own the motherfucking place . . .

Walking into his newly renovated kitchen, Shaft is like a jumpy and unsure jungle cat. Shaft scratches his huge, distended belly, and reaches toward the coffee machine, flicks on POWER, then takes a seat in his special chair: LET'S GO REDSKINS! sticker on the back, #1 DAD on the front.

Shaft grabs hold of his half-moon bifocals, the pair strung around his neck, slips them farther up his nose.

He grabs the paper, grabs it hard. The sports pages first . . . missing?

"Baby . . . baby, you see them sports pages?" asks Shaft. He reaches over for a slice of Entenmann's apple-crumb coffee cake (sinfully delicious).

"Have to leave," says Cokey, the woman of the household. "Getting my pants altered. Then over to the day spa. Cokey gonna pamper Cokey."

Shaft slams his fist down onto the table, and his coffee mug (PUBLIC TELEVISION, 25 YEARS!) leaps high into the air, coffee spilling onto the table, onto Shaft's pajamas, onto his slippers. And Shaft is repeating himself, this time louder, with the urgency of a Tribal Chief, to be feared, respected, honored.

"I said, woman, did you see them sports pages?"

Cokey laughs. "Got no time for your nonsense, Shaft."

"That's where you're wrong, baby," Shaft says. "You got a *lot* of time for my nonsense."

"Now why is that?" asks Cokey. "Now why should that be?"

"Because I got payoffs to make," says Shaft. "People to meet, taking care of business. Back in the weave."

"Sounds good," Cokey says. "Just remember that Zach finishes lacrosse practice in four hours. With you picking him up."

"Now just a minute, baby," says Shaft, licking the crumbs off his thick, powerful fingers. "Hold on for just one motherfucking minute. You didn't tell me nothin' about picking him up today. What you said was tomorrow. Pick him up tomorrow, is what you said."

"Baby shit," Cokey replied, laughing, slipping on the nylon Prada Carefree coat, $450 at the Montgomery Mall Nordstrom, shiny as all get-out, primavera green, for both summer and spring, versatile, durable, waterproof. "A retired man like yourself, still playing the game. You got your four hours."

"Woman—" Shaft begins, following her.

"Good-bye," Cokey continues.

"Yes, my love," Shaft finishes, gently.

☛ ☛ ☛

Shaft flicks on the radio. Shaft is in the mood to hear the slow jams. Not too hard, not too soft, that'll do just fine. Shaft sings along to the tunes, mouth moving beautifully in time. Shaft beats his fingers down on the steering wheel. Shaft checks himself out in the mirror and adjusts his IS IT FRIDAY YET? baseball cap.

"Lookin' fine," he mumbles to himself. "Goddamn fine."

Shaft stares out the driver's-side window of the minivan. But what's this? Could it be?

"Son of a bitch!" Shaft screams.

25 . . . 30 . . . 35 . . . 40 mph . . .

"Pull the fuck over!" Shaft screams, motioning toward the side of the road. "Honky, pull the fuck over!"

40 . . . 45 . . . 50 . . . 55 mph . . .

Shaft is directly behind Honky now, refusing to let him escape. Honky increases his speed, and Shaft, too, picks up speed. Both are up to 60 mph now, keeping solid pace with the rest of the highway traffic.

Beads of sweat form on Shaft's forehead, then drip down onto his khaki slacks. Shaft makes a mental note to have them dry-cleaned . . . and only one goddamn week since he last had them cleaned.

Shaft again motions for Honky to pull the fuck over, and to pull over right now! Honky rolls his eyes and does as he's asked. Shaft follows Honky, braking to a quick, hard stop, and flicking on his blinking hazards.

And then, in a flash, Shaft is exiting the minivan and sidling up to Honky's car.

"Roll down the window," barks Shaft, scratching his belly. "Roll down that damn window!"

"Let me guess," says Honky, sighing. "You want to borrow the sit-down mower. Again."

"Motherfucking right I do," says Shaft, striking a karate pose and then grimacing.

"Not a problem," says Honky. "How about in a few weeks?"

"Kind of need it now," says Shaft, rubbing his bad knee. "Lawn's not looking too good."

"We'll see what we can do," says Honky, starting the engine. "See what we can do."

"Now just a minute, friend," says Shaft, taking off his cap. "In-laws are stopping by next week. Kind of need it now."

"Give me a call," says Honky, pulling away. "Give me a ring and we'll chat."

"Now just a—" Shaft begins, attempting to run after him.

"A call," Honky shouts, pulling away.

"Sounds real good, Honky," Shaft finishes, coming to a slow and painful stop with both hands on his knees. "Real good."

☞ ☞ ☞

Shaft is back in the thick of it again. Shaft has work to do now, and he is anxious, like a jaguar on the prowl. Shaft is making his way through this new badass landscape, three hours to take care of business, doing it his way, no one else's, time goes by so quickly . . .

The hardware store, the stamps, the bag of mulch

for the rosebushes, back onto Falls Road, at the height of the midday traffic, to the lacrosse fields and Zach, only so much a man can do alone, with three hours to do it, not much time at all.

He thinks: There is so much to do . . . so much to accomplish . . . *Without having to wait in a goddamn grocery line.*

"What in the fuck is the tie-up?" screams Shaft, pushing the cart back and forth, back and forth, back and forth. "Ten items or less, right? C'mon, motherfuckers! Takin' care of business!"

Shaft takes a great big slurp from his container of raspberry Go-GURT. Shaft glances at his watch. He looks toward the front of the line.

"Let's go!" Shaft screams to the woman at the register. "Got errands! Think about that!"

"My Lord," says the teenager. "What now?"

"Errands," says Shaft, softer now.

"You will wait," finishes the teenager, annoyed. "You will wait just like anyone else."

"And so I shall," declares Shaft, even more softly. "And so I shall."

Shaft ignores the pointed looks. Ignores the heated stares. Shaft takes a tiny lick from the spilled yogurt that runs across his thick, powerful fingers. And then, to himself, mumbling: "Like a dangerous wild animal."

And then another lick.

"Like a dangerous motherfuckin' animal."

NEXT . . .

Chapter Two: "Cuttin' and Prunin' and Weedin' His Own Goddamn Way"

A Few Things I've Discovered about Teenagers

Rubbing balm on my pre-arthritic knees
ain't exactly "cool."

•

Also, they're not exactly too "keen" on touching my bald
spot with their bare feet.

•

In a similar vein, they are not hugely eager to scratch
beneath my carpal tunnel splints.

•

Deathly afraid of quicksand!

Really don't laugh at my impression of Dionne Warwick.
Surprisingly, not even just a little.

•

Could be a *BIT* more patient when it comes to my
14-year-old bulldog's spastic colon.

•

Not really into that "breaking into doo wop" thing.

•

Giving my ol' tootsies a spit shine ain't
exactly on their "To Do" list.

•

Simply adore muffins, just outta the oven.

•

As far as "hip" quotients go, "hugging sessions" that
take place beneath the bridge, down by the river, are
right up there with having a chat with a thirtysomething
guy in a food court about clothes, pop music, and
other teenage concerns, such as nude Twister. In other
words, most likely not very hip.

The Ongoing, Insanely Exciting Adventures of the Apple Valley High Gang!

(Costarring Tobi, the Wondrous Sleuth Pooch)

Volume 29 (of 36): Free Mumia!

AT THE BANANA HUT . . .

It was Friday afternoon and Cindi was once again in love.

"I'm in love," said Cindi, softly. "I'm in love, I'm in love, I'm in love!"

"Really?" asked Dani, sarcastically. She took a bite from a french fry and then continued: "Who is it this time? Johnny? Billy? Or how about Ricky? Take your pick!" She rolled her eyes, and then absentmindedly took a sip from her strawberry milkshake.

Tobi the sleuth pooch, who had previously been asleep on the floor, suddenly awoke with a loud bark. He, too, knew Cindi's history with boyfriends, and couldn't help but get in his own two cents. He then fell back asleep.

"None of the above!" answered Cindi. "It's a . . . secret."

The Apple Valley High Gang, not counting Cindi, gave each other a knowing look, and then went back to their meals. School had just let out for the day, but a lot of things were still on their minds. Like what present to buy for Mr. Charles, Apple Valley High's janitor, for his 30th birthday. Or what yummy dish to prepare for the charity dinner being thrown by the Apple Valley Chapter of the Muscular Dystrophy Association™, a most worthy cause, to be sure. But this? Forget it. Like all of Cindi's numerous crushes, this one would most likely fade . . . more quickly than Cindi probably realized.

"Can you spare all of us the suspense?" asked Sylvia, chewing on a piece of grape gum (as usual).

Cindi thought for a short while, and then sighed. "I suppose it's no use, as you'll all find out soon enough anyway. So here goes: It's Mumia."

Just one name was all it took. The Apple Valley High Gang groaned. Mumia? Why not pick the King of England or the Richest Man in the Universe? First of all, Mumia was an absolute perfect dreamboat. Second, he was already taken . . . he just had to be. Right?

Cindi pushed her long flowing red hair off her shoulders. Her gorgeous green eyes sparkled, and she let out a shy laugh.

"I . . . just can't get him off my mind," she said, poking at her pile of mashed potatoes with her fork, and pointing to Mumia's website on her orange laptop. "What can I really say—"

"That you're acting silly?" interjected Rachelle, between bites of apple pie and vanilla ice cream. "That there's not a chance in Apple Valley that you'll ever meet, let alone date, this gorgeous human being?"

Rachelle was just being honest. Within the group, she was known as the honest one. Sometimes *too* honest. The previous summer, while on vacation, Rachelle had inadvertently come across a pile of incriminating papers belonging to her father, a fireman. Although it had been an extremely difficult decision, Rachelle had immediately turned the papers over to a judge. Her father was subsequently arrested and, three years later, was still languishing in a prison somewhere in the Cayman Islands. [**Apple Valley High #13:** *Fire, Fire, Burning Bright*]

"She's right," interjected Dani, smiling. Her smile was warm and large. Over the years, it had melted many a young man's heart, including, but not limited to, Rudolf Giuseppe, the handsome, eldest son of an Italian count. Dani had fallen madly, head over heels in love with Rudolf, but Rudolf had died tragically in a snowmobile accident a few hours after they had met, thus dashing any hope that Dani might have had for the perfect prom. And that had been that. Until a few hours later, when she had met "Magic" Alex Shoumanoff, the gorgeous, brilliant son of a world-famous German opera singer. [**Apple Valley High #26:** *Les Dreams*]

Cindi, now slightly irritated by her friend's behavior, continued: "I need your help because it seems that Mumia needs *our* help." She rushed the words out, as if in a great hurry.

"What sort of help?" asked Sylvia, blowing a huge bubble.

"Yeah," asked Rachelle, "what sort of help could

Mumia *possibly* need from us, the Apple Valley High Gang?"

Cindi paused, and then exclaimed: "Why don't we just let Mumia tell us for himself?"

Sylvia let out a small gasp. As did Sara, Rachelle, and Dani.

"T-t-t-talk to him?" stuttered Sylvia. "N-n-n-now?"

"Sure," said Cindi. "If not now, when?"

"Um, okay," replied Sylvia, nervously. "If you say so."

"But we have to wait for him to call us," said Cindi. "Which he will. In exactly: five seconds . . . four . . . three . . . two . . . one!"

With that, Cindi's pink cell phone rang. "Hello?," Cindy answered excitedly. "Is that you, Mumia? I'm going to put you on the special speakerphone." Cindi pressed the lime-green "speakerphone" button, and Mumia could now be heard, his voice ringing loud and clear throughout the Banana Hut:

"Am I talking to the Apple Valley High Gang? Are you all there?"

"Yes!" said the Apple Valley High Gang in unison. "We're all here!"

"Dynamite," said Mumia, confidently. "Ladies, my name is Mumia, and I am in a hint of trouble. Unfortunately, I am in no position to explain. But please, Apple Valley High Gang, you must trust me on this! Do you think that you can trust me?"

Cindi looked over to Sylvia, who looked over to Sarah, who looked over to Dani, who at last looked over to Rachelle. All five nodded their heads in unison. Tobi the sleuth pooch, feeling slightly left out, awoke with a start, and began to bark. He had never met Mumia, but if he had, he would have most definitely taken an instant liking to him.

"Yes!" they all proclaimed. "We can trust you!"

"Super," replied Mumia, his voice full and husky. "I need the Apple Valley High Gang to do a bit of sleuthing."

"Sleuthing?" asked Dani, intrigued. "Tell us more."

"Look for the Whitey," replied Mumia. "The Blue-Eyed Peckerwood with that look in his eye that says, You are going down. You are going away for good. Look for the Hay-Eater. The Georgia Cracker who stole my life and left me here to rot. The Frosted Devil who holds the pristine bullet that was stolen from the side of the road. The Bloated Marshmallow who took that bullet, and shot me right through the heart. And the Pink-Faced Charlie who laughs heartily at my misfortune. I need them all found. Apple Valley Gang, do you think that you can do that for Mumia?" **["My Thoughts," by Mumia Abu-Jamal, SCI Greene Press, Volume 14]**

"The Peckerwood?" asked Dani, inquisitively.

"Yes," said Mumia.

"The Bloated Marshmallow?" asked Cindi, curiously.

"That's correct," said Mumia.

"The Georgia Cracker?" asked Rachelle, perplexed.

"Bingo. And the Frosted Devil," said Mumia. "Find them all. Do it for Mumia. It's glorious to have you all on my side!"

Sylvia blushed. She imagined Mumia's handsome African-American face lighting up as he said this. Perhaps Cindi wasn't so crazy after all, she thought. Perhaps not so crazy in the least. And, in fact, perhaps she, too, was beginning to come down with a slight crush on this sexy, mysterious man. What was it about him? His wonderful smile? His charming phone manners? Sylvia did not know for sure, and yet she also did not much care. She and the rest of the Gang had their work cut out for them. And it was high time they got busy . . .

"That sounds fantastic, Mumia! Talk to you later!" exclaimed Cindi. She pressed the purple "off" button on her pink cell phone, and smiled.

"*Now* do you understand?," Cindi asked, positively glowing. "Isn't he just the most?"

"Is he ever!" exclaimed Sara, standing up from the table. "Let's get sleuthing. For Mumia!"

The rest of the Apple Valley High Gang stood up from the table. Tobi, the wondrous sleuth pooch, also stood up. He knew it was time to go and he was very happy. Sylvia placed a miniature baseball cap onto his head, and he barked joyfully. This was all very exciting!

"To us!" screamed the Gang in unison, as they joined their hands together and then lifted them high into the air. "And to Mumia!"

Let the sleuthing begin!

NEXT . . .

Volume 30 (of 36): "Creating the MySpace Page . . ."

Kama Sutra: The Corrections

Page 97: The illustration of a couple engaged in
"Congress of the Cow" misidentifies the participants.
The male is "Rich Prince" (not Richard Prince from
Highland, Illinois) and the female is "Compliant
Servant" (not "Cynthia Servantés from Cincinnati,
Ohio"). We regret the errors.

Page 171: In the diagram that depicts the fourth-
century "Rocking Tortoise of the Kama Sutra,"
the male should be declaring, "In the realm of the
pleasurable, we are now both as one; together we
shall reach limits of ecstasy never before thought
imaginable," and not "Shit-damn, woman, you are
freakin' fine!"

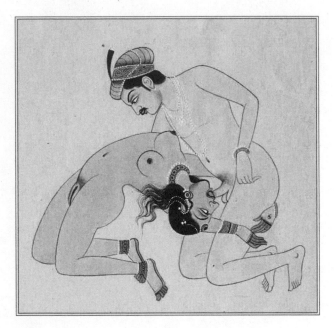

Page 29: The caption for "Giving Pleasure in the Back of the 7 Train" failed to mention that the subway train should have come to a full stop before one attempts this act, and that, while not in violation of any known statute, this maneuver will most likely be frowned upon if performed in front of tourists, the infirm, or groups of children on field trips to the local zoo.

Page 46: Due to a printer's error, the
following warning for "Pushing the
Wheelbarrow" was inadvertently omitted:
Do not under any circumstances deploy
this position as an "icebreaker" during first
dates, high-school reunions, or corporate-
retreat "Gettin' to Know Ya" seminars.

Page 52: "Splitting the Long Bamboo" requires the collaboration of seven people, not just one with a mirror. We apologize for any hemorrhaging that may have resulted.

Page 213: In "Mimicking Animals in Nature,"
please substitute "exotic Asiatic lions" for
"next-door-neighbors in rented Halloween
costumes doing it on their front lawn."

In the Author's Dedication, the phrase "To
my loving and beautiful wife, Narendra"
should have read: "To my loving and
beautiful and infinitely more limber second
wife, Savita."

Substitute Buddha Master

(Week Five: "Fire & Ice")

ME: Master, how does one find the strength within himself to find true love?

MY MASTER: By being one with the world that is without himself.

ME: How so?

MY MASTER: When fire meets ice, what prevails?

ME: Ice.

MY MASTER: Yet in dying, does not the ice in the fire also die?

ME: Um . . . I don't . . . could you possibly attack it from a different angle? I'm a little confused, my master.

MY MASTER (very angry): Did you not read the handout from last week?

ME: I am ashamed and dishonored to tell you that I have not.

MY MASTER: Spent a lot of money Xeroxing those for you.

ME: It's just that I had to pull that extra shift, and then one of the kids . . .

MY MASTER (exasperated): Is love not a reality that exists within all creatures?

ME: It is.

MY MASTER: And is love not a by-product of Heaven?

ME: This is correct.

MY MASTER: So does it not come to pass that this Heaven that we speak of . . . this Heaven that we . . . Jesus, what the fuck was I thinking before? You're messing with my head.

ME: That this Heaven is ours for the taking—

MY MASTER: Right. That this Heaven that we speak of is available to creatures both large and small?

ME: I think so—

MY MASTER: The answer is yes! Remember? The blackboard? The diorama? The giant wood pointer? The PowerPoint presentation? Did you not take notes? Has Master Sogyal Gangchen not taught you this stuff? By the way, where is that ass? Still out with a pulled groin, I imagine.

ME: Master—

MY MASTER: Yes or no? Did you not take notes?

ME: No.

MY MASTER: Thought so. Pathetic.

ME: But how can Heaven and Earth both reside within ourselves when—

MY MASTER: When they consist of two different realities?

ME: Yes.

MY MASTER: I knew you were going to ask me that stupid question. Um . . . I do know that Heaven lies within. Or is it without? Wait a second—see, you confused me again.

216 | MIKE SACKS

ME: And it is our earthly duties—

MY MASTER: I said, hang on a sec! Have you seen my book with all the answers?

ME: I'm not sure . . .

MY MASTER: It says "Life: Master's Edition" on the cover and on the back: "Not For Resale." I swear to God, if any one of you jackasses . . .

ME: Master, may I again talk of love?

MY MASTER: Make it quick. I have another class at the temple across town.

ME: If ice does indeed prevail from its meeting with fire, then why is ice not a more powerful element?

MY MASTER: I'm very hungry and dinner beckons, a dinner that I shall consume in my RAV4. So I'll tell you what: try a little experiment, a homework assignment of sorts. Go home. Take some ice. Light it on fire. Write down what happens. We'll discuss it next week. Sound good?

ME: But have we not already decided tha—

MY MASTER: Am I a joke to you?

ME: Master?

MY MASTER: I didn't go to Buddhist school, and

I don't have a diploma. I never did attend a fancy
Buddhist retreat on top of a big ol' mountain. I wear
a bald rubber cap to look smart, and fake glasses to
appear wise. This makes me a joke?

ME: No, master. But . . . as for this question of love—

MY MASTER: Ahhhh, if I didn't need the money so
bad . . . (sadly, to self) You make one wrong turn in life,
money troubles, women troubles, government troubles
. . . twenty years down the road, you take a long look
in the mirror, and guess what you see? An enlightened
bodhisattva. How the hell did that happen, you think?
Oh, man.

ME: And Heaven?

MY MASTER: You . . . you ask me that stupid question
one more time, so help me! *I. Do. Not.* Know. *Capisce?*

ME: Maybe next week?

MY MASTER: Maybe. By the way, bloodstains on a
robe. Laundering advice?

Answer to Last Week's Zen Koan:

The grasshopper knew the ant from just seeing him
around; that was why he did not harm him.

Worst Places to Die

In your attic, crushed under the weight of your
vintage erotica collection

•

At the head of a conga line in the Mexican section
of Busch Gardens

•

Crouched in the rafters above the high-school girls'
locker room, your janitorial uniform bunched
around your ankles

Instants before the flash explodes on that
whimsical "old-timey" photo

•

Roughly six minutes after mumbling, "What's the worst
that can happen?" and stopping to pick up that drifter
with the "colorful past"

•

Prepped and ready for your first-ever high colonic

•

In the cougar pen at the Bronx Zoo, gingerly
retrieving your Swatch

•

In your garage, whimsically whipping up your
first homemade batch of meth from a recipe you
found on Craigslist

•

Pinned beneath a huge boulder, just after amputating
your left arm, much closer to civilization than you
previously thought

•

On the red-eye, somewhere over Kansas, a copy of
Hemispheres on your lap

•

In the media room at the local public library, just
having Googled "herpes + cure???"

•

In a "high-end" Porta-John

•

On some asshole's new sailboat

At a comic-book convention, play-wrestling with
"The Incredible Hulk"

•

Onstage at an acting workshop, just having
grabbed the "improv baton"

•

Naked in a stolen paddleboat

•

In a puddle of urine, not your own

•

Lying prone before a congregation of the "Alternative
Church" you stumbled upon in the woods

•

At a gang-bang-video shoot, with a sign taped to
your back that reads "Participant #126"

•

In the arms of a talking tree after gorging on
Jimsonweed

•

Halfway through your shift passing out flyers
in that giant-pickle costume

•

In the back room of Spencer Gifts, fiddlin' with the
candles shaped like penises

•

Slow-dancing in your living room, alone, to
Chris de Burgh's "The Lady in Red"

Williamsburg, Virginia: tricornered hat,
head in the stocks

•

In line for a funnel cake

•

At the company Halloween party, dressed
as a secondary sex characteristic

•

In the midst of a boot-scootin' line dance

•

Strapped into your rented parasail on a Bahamas
beach, doing the "look, no hands!" move for the
woman you just met from Long Island

•

Between the letters *H* and *J* while licking
the alphabet "down there"

•

Arriving stag at your thirty-fifth high-school reunion,
taking that last step out of your rented stretch SUV

•

In your apartment, with AC/DC's "Big Balls"
blasting from the stereo, set to "repeat"

•

On a toilet in a Barnes & Noble bathroom,
reading this book

Funny Letters from Summer Camp and Their Not-So-Funny Responses

Dear Mummy and Daddy:

Camp is fun and I'm eating a lot of candy!!! Kevin today caught a frog and it climbed into his shirt!

Todd

Dear Todd:

Mummy and I are getting a divorce. Will give you specifics when you come home. Tell Kevin's frog we say hi!

Mummy and Daddy

Dad and Mom:

Yesterday I went swimming for six hours and when
I got out of the water I was all wrinkly!!! Walter my
bunkmate threw up after eating a whole pizza. Before
lights out yesterday we all sang "101 Bottles of Beer." I
fell asleep before it was done!

Chris

Dear Chris:

It's funny you should mention "throwing up" and "beer,"
sweetheart. Mommy won't be visiting this weekend. Do
you like this special hospital stationery? Don't get too
wrinkly now or you'll turn into a prune!

Daddy

Dear Mom:

Yesterday—wait, two days ago—I got into the best
adventure of my entire life! We started off running
to the springs where we ran around and around and
ate lunch. And then I climbed a tree and then I killed
a bug with my shoe and then we went back and had
dinner. I won the skit contest. It was the best day of
my entire life! I will never ever ever ever ever forget
it!!!!!!!!!!!!!!!!!!!!!

Kim

☞ Return to sender, no forwarding address

Dear Mom n Dad!

4got to send U a letter bee-4. R U having as much fun as eye am having? Wink.

Katy

P.S.—Do U get it?

Katy:

UR brother is dead. He 4-got to put on his motorcycle helm-8. C U very soon, K-8-ty!

Mom and Dad

P.S. Of course we get it, why wouldn't we? The joke was obvious, really.

O, Matty Parker: My Roommate, My Patron!

O, Matty Parker of Manhattan! I sing your praises as your official historian and biographer! The magnificence of your existence knows no bounds!

(As you already know from having read the previous 253 chapters, this is the ongoing biography of my roommate and patron, Matty Parker, 31, of Manhattan. In lieu of paying for rent or food, I spend my days and nights following Matty around, and then—usually very late in the evening, after Matty has gone to bed—I type up and e-mail a brand-new chapter to all of you.)

What follows is Chapter 254, which I shall call "March 26." It was a very busy and fulfilling day!

Matty awakes at noon.

At precisely 2:05 PM, Matty meets with his former wife in the "Self Help" section of the Book Nook, near Lincoln Center, to iron out some details pertaining to the divorce settlement. The meeting ends with the somewhat sudden departure of Matty's wife at 2:07 PM.

After apologizing to the store's staff for losing his temper and trying to rip in half *Understanding Ourselves & Our Relationships*, Matty makes his way over to Gray's Papaya—at the corner of 72nd Street and Broadway—for a delicious, relaxing lunch.

Matty orders his usual: a large hot dog topped with coleslaw and extra mustard. While waiting for his order, Matty chats up a new employee, a pretty blonde working the cash register. Although the conversation starts slowly, Matty quickly impresses her with a detailed joke about a shy nun and a very randy sailor. As is his custom, Matty acts out all of the roles, complete with special vocal inflections and nuanced gestures.

Lunch ends at 2:40 PM, just after Matty explains to the restaurant's manager that making seventeen-year-olds cry is not necessarily a hobby of his.

At 2:46 PM, Matty finishes his hot dog out on the sidewalk.

At 2:48 PM, Matty generously feeds a squirrel the remains of his bun.

As luck would have it, an old acquaintance of Matty's happens to then pass by, Jill Turner, whom Matty has not seen in many years. After some pleasantries, the conversation continues thus:

Jill: "So, who's your friend? And why is he jotting down everything you're saying?"

Matty: "That's my roommate. He's under my patronage."

Jill: "Patronage?"

Matty: "I once read a *Prince Valiant* comic strip about a king who had his very own writer, and I thought it would be cool to have one also."

At 3:09 PM, Jill leaves somewhat suddenly.

At 3:47 PM, Matty purchases a very nice pair of striped slacks that will be more than adequate for an interview with a temp agency. Let me stress once again that Matty shouldn't be held accountable for losing his last job! How Matty was accused of masturbating in the office's technology room remains a mystery and will not be spoken of further, at least in this chapter. (For additional information, please see Chapter 186: "Matty is Escorted Out of Merrill Lynch by a Double-Gloved Security Guard.")

At 4:15 PM, Matty reads the entire Help Wanted section of *The New York Times* while standing at a magazine/ newspaper kiosk, paying particularly close attention to those jobs that won't require references.

A detailed account of the next five minutes:

4:17 PM: Matty steps in a wad of gum.

4:21 PM: Matty claps an old man on the back.

4:21 PM: Old man tells Matty not to touch him.

4:21 PM: Matty says he meant no disrespect; he was just trying to be friendly.

4:22 PM: Old man spits.

With much already accomplished, it is now time to head home!

As Matty and I walk back to our apartment, I take a moment to recall some of my all-time favorite "Matty-isms," deliciously witty quips and one-liners that Matty is so justifiably famous for.

Here are just a few:

"If owning a tanning lamp is a luxury, then call me luxurious." (November 3)

"The heavier the cologne, the louder she's gonna moan." (February 15)

"Flavored popcorn is for assholes." (often)

"If there's a better party song than 'Kokomo,' I'd like to know about it." (March 3)

"Superheroes who fly get laid the *most*. Superheroes who swim get laid the *least*." (Unknown)

"If I wore a bathing suit with horizontal stripes, would my penis appear larger?" (March 12)

(Note: There are literally thousands upon thousands of "Matty-isms," all of which you can find in **Appendix A** of this book.)

By 5:21 PM, Matty is safely ensconced back in his "Poon Shack," the three-bedroom condo on West 79th that he bought a few years ago with a little help from his extraordinarily successful father (whom Matty resembles in both looks and character, if not height and personality). This is when things *really* heat up . . .

- A magnificent and delicious dinner begins at 6:21 PM, with the arrival of the deliveryman from Señor Swanky's bearing the "Jalapeno Fire Bombs."

- At 6:33 PM, Matty finishes drinking his fourth margarita out of a large plastic mug in the shape of a festive sombrero.

- At 7:35 PM, Matty vomits into his large, sombrero-shaped plastic mug.

As I now (at 9:45 PM) watch Matty slowly and begrudgingly finish his Mexican food sans utensils, I take a quick moment to thank myself for having responded to that full-page ad he placed in the back of *The Village Voice* in March 2010. The fact that I had just graduated from NYU, and couldn't afford to pay the rent on any apartment in Manhattan, let alone on such a beautiful one on the Upper East Side, only furthers my admiration for this amazing human being!

Meanwhile, Matty burps loudly, yet not obnoxiously. This can signify only one thing: that Matty is readying himself for bed.

"Catch you on the rebound," he impishly declares, winking and then making his way into his spacious bedroom, decorated just so with numerous and exciting promotional bar freebies. (For a complete and alphabetized list, please check out **Appendix B**.)

Looking after Matty with awe, and wiping the hot sauce off my hand with a paper napkin, I can't help but smile. If day 254 was this exciting, what will day 255 have in store? Another old man spitting? Or perhaps just a quiet and rewarding day of "ordering in" and listening to Matty karaoke by himself to his enormous collection of *Party Jamz* CDs? No matter how it plays out, at least until my student loans are paid off, I'll be along for the exhilarating ride!

O, Matty Parker, my roommate and my patron, I shall continue to sing your praises, as you are unequivocally without equal! Until tomorrow's electrifying chapter, I am very truly yours . . .

Mike Sacks,
Official Biographer of Matty R. Parker,
He of the Upper East Side of Manhattan

Happiness Is . . .

. . . head to toe in latex, and two free hours in
"the coffin."

•

. . . rubbing a snow cone on your tummy, and screaming,
"All aboard the LOVE BOAT!"

•

. . . regaining consciousness in a tricked-out van on
I-270 and meeting your "Internet friend" for the very
first time.

. . . hot-tubbing with your homeboys, two of whom are leaving for chiropractic school in the spring.

•

. . . emerging from your break-dancing lessons into the early-afternoon sunshine, your sexy rattail tickling your tightly clenched ass. You've just nicknamed yourself "Buzzy."

•

. . . wearing cutoff "clam-diggers" and a straw hat, shooting acorns at the authorities with a homemade slingshot.

•

. . . 10:45 PM. A coffee enema and a heaping slice of microwavable apple pie. Then: bed.

•

. . . comparing scars at a family reunion.

•

. . . after a difficult day at the office, releasing your bladder on the M-66 crosstown bus, and impishly declaring: "As a *New Yorker* wag once quipped: 'When God gives you lemons . . . '"

•

. . . sitting in a tall tree, playing a pennywhistle.

•

. . . delighting in the rainbow prisms of light reflecting off the broken bottle being brandished in your face by a lovable stewbum.

Happiness Isn't . . .

. . . the smell of your hair after fourteen hours in
my homemade "sweat lodge."

•

. . . what you once did to my sandwich.

•

. . . a horseradish facial mask.

•

. . . your *Star Wars*–themed bedroom aids.

. . . using "Velveeta" as your S&M safe word.

•

. . . a man in a trench coat nicknamed "Mister Sads."

•

. . . that tattoo of Yosemite Sam next to your anus, screaming "Come on out of your hole, varmint!"

•

. . . being forced to take part in your boss's daughter's "deflowering ceremony."

•

. . . a moldy peach stuffed in a tube sock and left on my windowsill as a token of friendship.

•

. . . a three-way with you, me, and that dim-witted bagger from the Piggly Wiggly.

•

. . . Grandpa's famous shin massage.

•

. . . what I just left in your garden.

Contract for Your Appearance on *Worst Family in the World*

THIS APPEARANCE AGREEMENT, dated as of
_____, is being entered into by and
between GRAND EXPLOITS PRODUCTIONS LLC
("Producers") and HARRIS and GENEVIEVE CAMPBELL
(representatives of "The Campbell Family" and
Legal Guardians of the children BEN and COLLEEN
CAMPBELL) in reference to The Campbell Family's
appearance on the reality-television program, THE
WORST FAMILY IN THE WORLD.

1. The Campbell Family represents and warrants
that they are a legally recognized family unit bound

by immediate blood relation or legal adoption. Should it be discovered during the term of this agreement that a member of The Campbell Family has a heretofore undisclosed "secret" family, or that any of the Campbell children were obtained through illegal means, including black-market purchase, kidnapping from competing reality program(s), and/or illegal cloning experimentation conducted by non-sanctioned scientists, the Producers reserve the right to broadcast these revelations and integrate them into "Story."

2. The Campbell Family represents and warrants that, as far as they are aware, they constitute the worst family in the known world; that all members of Family are willing to exploit the family bond and inflict long-term emotional harm on each other in exchange for a brief moment in the pop-culture spotlight, lasting no longer than three (3) weeks or one (1) *Tonight Show* mention. Whether or not the Campbell Children ("Children") are capable of grasping the long-term damage to their psyches that could result from their appearance on Program is immaterial to the scope of this agreement.

3. The Campbell Family represents and warrants that Harris Campbell is a chronically underemployed sociopath incapable of establishing an emotional bond with anyone within or without the Family, whose parenting skills would shame most prairie wolves; that Harris Campbell is an aspiring bounty hunter who hopes to use his appearance on Program to launch his own, family-oriented bounty hunter business, THE CATCH 'EM CAMPBELLS INCORPORATED, which would have the entire Campbell family engage in fugitive apprehension and detainment as a family unit.

4. The Campbell Family will not be provided with protective gear (specifically but not limited to helmets, bulletproof vests, bomb-squad uniforms, camouflage jackets) unless said gear incorporates the logo of "The Worst Family in the World" in bright pink (heretofore to be copyrighted as "Campbell Family Pink").

5. The Campbell Family represents and warrants that Genevieve Campbell is on a regimen of numerous psychotropic medications, both prescribed and otherwise, including home-brewed, and that the dosage instructions for these medications are often taken as "suggestions"; that since the age of twenty-six (26), Genevieve Campbell has never made a decision for herself or for her family that wasn't an overt and direct rebuke to her own father (whereabouts unknown); that Genevieve Campbell will spend most of her screen time on said Program spouting shrill platitudes about the importance of family; that Genevieve Campbell once went eight months without speaking to either of her two (2) children to prove, in her words, "that they need *me* more than I need *them*."

6. The Campbell Family represents and warrants that Colleen Campbell is sixteen (16) years old, as indicated on the birth certificate surrendered to Producers; that by commonly accepted standards, Colleen Campbell is very promiscuous for her age; that as far as either parent is aware, Colleen Campbell is not presently pregnant, despite appearances and medical tests to prove otherwise; that both parents agree that if Colleen is pregnant, or should become pregnant during taping of Program, the decision of whether or not to terminate pregnancy will be left to the sole discretion of Producers, in conjunction with call-in/online voting of viewing audience.

7. The Campbell Family represents and warrants that Ben Campbell is twelve (12) years old, as indicated on the birth certificate surrendered to Producers; that Ben Campbell is presently serving a six-month sentence of juvenile probation for setting fire to several neighborhood households; that psychiatric therapy for Ben Campbell has been temporarily suspended, as the Campbell Family think the money will be better spent to enroll Ben in a nine-week Cha-Cha Slide class, in anticipation of his crossover appearance on a reality dance show to be determined upon removal of his home-detention anklet.

8. Statement of Intent. The Campbell Family intends, to the best of their ability, to conduct themselves and all Family interactions in a manner that puts the entertainment of the viewing audience above the private concerns of Family at all times; to never engage in any Activity that is not being captured on camera ("Activity" should encompass kinetic activity, such as physical interaction and conversation, as well as internal activity, such as quiet thought, introspection, dwelling upon long-abandoned hopes and dreams, and digestion).

9. Consent To Participation In Challenges. The Campbell Family gives consent for the entire Family to participate in on-screen Program Challenges, including "Family Whitewater Raft Race," "Family Hang-glide Dogfight," "Don't You Dare Bring That Up," "72 Hours in the Hole," "I Bet I Can Make You Weep," and "Family Cross-Country Hitchhike Adventure."

10. Elimination. The Campbell Family agrees that at end of initial season, whichever family member is "voted off" will agree to a legal separation from the family unit, and will avoid all contact with family members until there has elapsed a period of eighteen (18) months or two (2) *SNL* mentions, or production begins on a "The Worst Family in the World" Reunion Special, whichever event occurs sooner.

11. Indemnification. The Campbell Family shall indemnify and hold harmless Producers for any injury or damages suffered during production of Program, including, but not limited to dehydration, skin irritation, amnesia brought on by induced disorientation, gunshot wounds, drowning, insanity, loss of limbs, loss of wits, loss of genitals, unstoppable hiccupping, hyena-like laughing, unprompted screaming, episodes of delirium lasting for more than eight (8) months, or any other phobia(s) resulting from live burial.

Your signature on this notarized agreement (in Campbell Family Pink) effectively bestows upon your family eligibility to appear on THE WORST FAMILY IN THE WORLD.

Signed,

_____   _____

_____   _____

Campbell Family

_____   _____

Producers

Director's Commentary

Hello, I'm director Eric Wenger, pleased to be here providing commentary for the twentieth-anniversary DVD re-release of *Daniel Kaufman's Bar Mitzvah Video: The Director's Cut*.

Boy, this takes me back! August 1990: I was three months out of SUNY Purchase film school, broke and living in the basement of my aunt's house in Hoboken, and I suppose the Kaufmans, old family friends, did me a favor. Our troubles really began in that heated pre-production meeting in their kitchenette.

I suggested we shoot on a Northern California mountaintop at the golden hour, for that lush Terrence Malick cinematography. The Kaufmans were difficult, and booked a Forest Hills synagogue on a Saturday morning. I wanted something Bergman-esque— allegorical, full of religiosity, muted Scandinavian chiaroscuro. They preferred a derivative remake of their neighbor Jessica Cohen's rather mainstream Bat Mitzvah video. I was set to attach a taller, blonder actor for the lead—preferably a Gentile. They insisted on their own son. One makes concessions, that's all.

Oh, *this* scene! It took me hours to get it just right: a long, slow tracking shot through the window and then up to the dais, where Daniel stands reciting from the Torah—an homage to Welles's *Touch of Evil*, but also to *Ernest Goes to Camp*. Knocking down the protagonist with the camera was completely improvised, but I kept it in; it just felt *true*. Look at the anguished expression on Daniel's face as he hits the ground—very Peckinpah, with just the slightest dash of the Wayans brothers' *Little Man*.

By the way, I had most of Daniel's dialogue and speeches punched up by a script doctor in postproduction. That would account for some of the dubbing problems, as well as the references to "following your heart" and the catchphrase "It's Torah time!"—which, perhaps not surprisingly, failed to catch on with the 'tween audience.

Does the subplot work, the one between Rabbi Horwitz and the beautiful call girl with a potentially dangerous secret? The secret was that she was sleeping with the cantor. Can't tell . . .

Can you make out Daniel's grandfather sitting in the front row? The elderly, wheelchair-bound man in the throes of spiritual ecstasy? Weeping softly, tenderly, with patriarchal love? Now, without warning, he's performing the hora all by himself in the aisle, and swinging his tallis overhead in the manner of Slim Pickens with his cowboy hat in *Dr. Strangelove*, or Billy Drago with his pickaxe in *The Hills Have Eyes*? I wasn't satisfied with the original take, so with the re-release I had that last bit computer-generated. Adds some drama and an homage to an otherwise flat mise-en-scène.

Also new is the hundred-person African-American choir leading the congregation with a gospel-tinged version of "Baruch Adonai."

Act III. I endlessly focus-grouped the climactic scene with various members of the Forest Hills Jewish Community Center. Should it be uplifting—perhaps the Bar Mitzvah boy triumphs over the synagogue bully by French-kissing the hottest girl in Hebrew school? Or tragic—Mrs. Kaufman succumbs in the rabbi's tan, loving arms from an unnamed terminal illness? I eventually went with my gut and with an ending that elegantly captured the Talmudic origins of *bar mitzvah*, meaning "one to whom the commandments apply."

So here comes the food fight. Certainly, I had Buster Keaton's deadpan sensibility in mind here, although, given the air of urbanity and cynical underpinning, one could surely make a case that it owes a greater debt to *Police Academy 4: Citizens on Patrol*. The theft of my tripod just before the shoot became a blessing in disguise—the handheld camera lends the scene some Cassavetes-style vérité, as does my audible cursing.

Sure, the critics later complained that the scene felt incongruous—and Mr. and Mrs. Kaufman never really "got" my artistic vision, either. They mostly appeared concerned with the dry-cleaning costs. And their son's concussion and dizzy spells. Difficult. Very difficult.

An aside for all you cinephiles: I also shot a controversial alternate ending in which Daniel angrily renounces Judaism, à la Peter Finch in *Network*. The Kaufmans "left it on the cutting-room floor," or, to be more precise, burned it in their backyard.

Wow, what a rite of passage this whole experience was for me as a director! Here are the title cards foretelling what happened to those involved with the film. The Kaufmans opted not to bankroll additional feature projects with me as auteur, and stopped returning my calls after I hand-delivered the original Betamax cassette.

But that's showbiz, ain't it? One year, you're the new Coppola; the next, you're substitute teaching at a high school and, on the side, operating your own infomercial production company, which recently won three "Mersh Awards" for its role in selling high-efficiency pasta cookers and nonstick skillets.

Am I proud of my work? Sure! Do I wish I'd done things differently? Of course. Which is why I'm currently meeting with investors about a sequel. Two decades later, and the filmmaking world has finally caught up to my aesthetic: Rapid-fire pop-culture banter! A nonlinear, multiple-POV narrative! More handsome, goyish characters. And, now that the actors are no longer minors, full-frontal nudity.

Thanks for listening. Have to get out of the AV room now. Back to class. Kickball today. See you around town—I'm often nursing a vanilla fizzy at Friendly's.

So . . . a little help shutting this goddamn contraption off?

Shared Beach House for Rent: Act QUICKLY!

$1,000 wk/8BR – Come enjoy beautiful East Hampton this summer! Awesome beach house just steps from ocean, with fabulous views throughout. New Weber grill. Plenty of rooms to sob in. Totally did not just rent this and hope I could find 7 other people to spend the summer with me. Tennis nearby. Minutes from town. Jacuzzi. Newly installed phone for late-night therapist and ambulance dialing. New bedding. Bedbug issue semi-resolved.

Other amenities include laundry room, weight room, a guy looking to meet some cool buds, wrap-around deck where the seeds of new friendships can be planted, showers no one has rigged to look at you naked, etc.

No smokers! Fresh ocean breezes and a kickin' stereo that will continuously blast bluegrass covers of Pink Floyd classics. There is also a white-noise machine to cancel out all sounds of real waves and children's laughter.

Free on-site parking, but you must be willing to drive me to bars and restaurants if you're headed there. FiOS, Bluetooth and Internet included—there are no filters, except when Googling my name. Just unpack and relax. Seriously. Almost like a cottage.

Fully stocked kitchen, but no tempting knives. I have a 25-foot boat, perfect for throwing parties and chillin'. Or just showing the locals that I do have friends. Library stocked with used self-help books that work with varying results.

Central air. Pets negotiable! Not negotiable: willingness to play board games. Also: a willingness to wear jammies and to sprinkle rainbow jimmies on everything!

Compulsory Goofy Golf championship held every third night. Winners must strut around porch with a homemade coconut trophy. Obligatory participation in nightly naked trust falls (or clothed, whatevs). Again, absolutely no smoking! But if you must, that's okay, too.

Very few rules! That said, if you do disobey the rules you will have to partake in impromptu tickling contests. RESERVE NOW! This one is too good to pass up!

To reiterate: you will NOT be disappointed with this house! Billy Joel's uncle once took a bowel movement in the bathroom. Hardwood floors throughout. Very effective vacuum cleaner. I am a great listener. Must be an expert at that Israeli paddle game and willing to teach me how to play. May take hours. May take days. May take all summer. Patience is a virtue. How can you resist?! Heated hot tub! 65-inch, black-and-white plasma TV! Must adore the movies of Meg Ryan— played at ear-deafening levels!

Lavish furnishings. House decorated in warm, natural beach tones. The recurring theme is that of being stuck on a desert island, with an ever-decreasing supply of water and sanity. Outdoor shower. Homemade soaps and shampoos available for purchase. Cash only. Leather-and-suede "L"-shaped couch, perfect for charades and heavy petting (or more), if everyone's comfortable and the mood is right. You've found heaven! SEARCH NO FURTHER!

Six Flags just 326 miles away.

Renters (new pals) only pay for electric, plumbing, cable, gas, as well as installation of solar panels to be attached to aforementioned jacuzzi. Refrigerator covered with "Wizard of Id" comics. Beach tags included—but required only inside house.

Must sneeze into the crook of your elbow. No shirt, no shoes, no underwear, no problem! No need to bring a large Betty Boop "Surf's Up" flag—I already have one. You know those extremely loud capiz-shell windsocks everyone hates? Have three of those. Enjoy your time fishing, crabbing, kayaking, Jet Skiing, or simply watching super-8 movies of me watching you sleep!

Beach chairs provided. Must be willing to assemble fifteen IKEA POÄNG beach chairs. Hey, folks! This house is one sweet, neat, complete retreat! Come and enjoy the windswept charm! Bike rack. Bocce equipment. Bring your own CPR kit. Just kick back, relax, and help me cover myself in Noxzema. In the evening, the sunsets will turn the sky pink, and our thoughts will turn to mandatory skit night (last weekend in August). Winner gets unlimited Eskimo kisses and alone time with owner.

Flexible check-in/check-out dates: June 3 before 9:00 AM, out on September 4 before 9:00 AM. Low $200 security deposit returned ASAP, on the compulsory condition that we have become inseparable.

So if you're looking for a fun vacation, close to the beach, with a guy with *extraordinarily* high expectations of what he needs from others, you've come to the perfect spot! What R U waiting for? Seriously. What? Contact owner for more information or just to say hi. Photos okay. Actually, photos would be great! Yeah! PHOTOS A MUST!

Baseball Boners!

(Post-Career)

Dropping the baby again.

•

Getting drunk and hitting your car with a bat,
but missing the side mirror.

•

Misreading the "You're fired" sign from your boss
as you round the hallway at top speed wearing nothing
but a tank top and a straw boater.

Sliding headfirst into a pyramid of soup cans in a
grocery store and breaking your leg.

•

Mistakenly spitting tobacco juice onto your cleats while
in a session with the marriage counselor.

•

Falling asleep on a pitching mound,
only to wake up to discover that your son's Little
League game is not today, but tomorrow.

•

Dying.

Famous Philosophers and
How They Were First Discovered

Anselm of Canterbury

Full-page promotional ad in local paper paid for by his
parents. Text written by his aunt, a professional writer
of sorts; she once penned an unpublished romance
novel.

Bernard of Clairvaux

Fucks like the wind. Loves like a dream.

Aristotle

Knew someone, who knew someone else, who knew the secrets of the universe. They got in touch. Still has his hair done by this man. The man's name? Mr. Weatherford.

Friedrich Wilhelm Nietzsche

Summer replacement for previous town philosopher. Stays for good.

Confucius

Edgy theories pertaining to life's great mysteries quickly adopted by fringe contingent. Slowly, carefully, moves into the mainstream. Not long thereafter deemed a "sellout." Q ratings drop. Rise. Remain steady. Now philosophizing part-time at the Dutch Apple Dinner Theater, Lancaster, PA.

Plato

Legally adopted at seventeen by sleazy manager type. Changes hairstyle, wardrobe. Grows dynamite handlebar mustache. Favorite hobby: "Spilling seed on rocks." Original name: Jacob Cohen.

Abelard

Large but proud nose distinguishes Abelard from the rest of the philosopher pack. Also: Sleepy-eyed and perpetually tanned. This kid is yummy.

Thomas Aquinas

Hung like a champ.

Francis Bacon

Colossal head of hair. Recently received calf implants.

René Descartes

Myth: Lover extraordinaire. Reality: Disaster in bed. At moment of climax, screams: "Little Pony!" Rumors spread. Those in the know are intrigued. Decide to find out for themselves. Within weeks, screams of "Little Pony!" can be heard across the canyon. And beyond.

John Locke

Child-philosopher prodigy, before forming the philosophizing duo of Locke & Load. Goes solo. Now rich as hell and can't give a hoot about all those jerkoff philosopher-impersonators gigging on the Vegas nightclub scene.

William of Ockham

This is an interesting story, I read about it in a magazine. I think it goes something like: William meets Hippocrates at a public bath. He shows him a scar shaped like a rose. Hippocrates is impressed enough to ask: "What do you want to do with your life?" "I want to philosophize." "Why?" is the response. "I want to help humanity." "You're an idiot." "Please, just give me this." "I'll see what I can pull." I'm forgetting the ending.

Jean-Paul Sartre

Discovered while eating a turkey hoagie and contemplating the meaning of life at a roadside stand. Also, admit it: he's cute as a goddamn bug!

Benedict Spinoza

Auditioned. Simple as that.

Albert Camus

Cleft chin makes all the ladies swoon. And the men? Forget it, he's a brother, a friend, a drinking buddy. That guy you want to hang around with during your off-time, not the brightest fella in the world, but non-threatening and quite partial to laughing at your jokes that involve geisha girls with ample, dimpled bottoms.

John Duns Scotus

Unknown.

Immanuel Kant

How was he discovered? Does it really matter? He is ultra-smooth and the public has little say in the matter. He is here for good. Get used to it.

Who is your favorite philosopher? What were they famous for? Do you like them a lot? What would you like to do with your life? There are so many questions, but so few answers.

My Family Home Movie: The 10th Anniversary

(Co-Starring Janeane Garofalo)

Back story:

Fifteen years ago, I invited Janeane Garofalo to appear
in my family's home movie. Although offered very little
money, she accepted readily, with only three conditions:
That we were to call her by her real name; that we were
to receive no outside funding from a major studio; and
that she was to be allowed to dress however she wished.
Easy. Done.

<u>Fifteen Years Ago</u>

CAST:

Mike Sacks (as himself, home from the big city for the weekend)

Mrs. Martha Sacks (as herself, the mother)

Mr. Robert Sacks (as himself, the father)

Janeane Garofalo (only sister, ironic, world-bent, deliciously cunning, never left home, everybody's favorite, except for the men, who unfortunately tend to overlook her in favor of her best friend, the beautiful, exotic Noelle. This is unfair, but little can be done about it, other than putting them all in their well-deserved places with an impeccably timed quip. She is sporting [in an arduously casual manner] a mocha tank top, olive-drab shorts, four thin, leather bracelets, two on each arm, and a leather cuff [right arm]. She is also sporting a pair of steel-toed black chukka boots. Her tattoos are many. She is different. She is wonderful. She is, for this afternoon, our wisecracking older sister/eldest daughter. We love her dearly.)

Cue-in ...

A screened-in porch. A table is laid end to end with a bounty of delicious food. The sun is setting. It is a typical scene of a typical family. It is dusk in Hopewell, Virginia, and all is well with the world. On a circular dinner table sits a red, green, and black candle that is shaped like a watermelon. For now, it is unlit.

Ext ...

Janeane enters from the left. She is scowling and holding her stomach.

Janeane: I feel all bright-eyed and mussy-furred, like a mangy dog ridden hard and put away wet. Do I look like a Tijuana rag doll to all of you? (Rolls eyes) The fucker gives me a call this morning, like I'm his cabana-girl bitch that he can just ring up whenever he feels the urge to merge. I pick up the phone and this is what I get. (Low, guttural voice) "Uh, yeah . . . like you're friends with Noelle, right? Okay, kind of wondering if you could hook me up with her, because she's like, more beautiful than you're ever going to be, so sorry." (Normal voice) And I'm thinking: "Hey, professor, go out and rut with a saucy wench and leave me out of it."

Martha: Sweetheart, you want one hot dog or two?

Janeane (picking up a raw hot dog): Looks familiar. Like a lady's lollipop just before the Viagra hits.

Robert: Hon, can we get her a drink?

Martha: Of course—

Janeane (sarcastically): Yeah, I need a drink like I need a hole in both your heads. By the way, what's with that T-shirt, daddy? Looks like something Mr. Disney would have pinched out.

Robert (laughing): You're funny!

Janeane: Funny? No. The only thing that I am is hungry. Where in the fuck is the food already?

Robert: Almost, almost. Anyone up for a game?

Mike: Sure.

Martha: Sure.

Janeane: Let me a tell you a story. It's about a family that's so lame they can think of nothing better to do than to play lousy games. Let me tell you another story: I feel like an Asian princess in a Greek fairy tale, bound and gagged, and then rolled over with my belly exposed. Okay, story done.

Voice of Mike (laughing): That was great!

Martha (laughing): Yeah, fantastic!

Robert (laughing): It's fun having you in our movie! We've never had a daughter. This is nice.

Janeane: What's with this house? Is the family allergic to black? And this watermelon candle? Where in the shit did you find this little gem? The gift shop in Hades?

Martha (laughing): At a garage sale on Windsor View. Isn't it darling? Let me light it.

Janeane: Christ damn. Okay, dig this: You're paying me to be here today, and I can respect that. I'm the older, wise-cracking sibling, that's fine. So I'll give you five more minutes and then I'll take my check and I'll leave.

Robert (laughing): Sounds good.

Martha (laughing): Okay.

Mike (laughing): Great.

Janeane (in a tight close-up): Okay, so here we go: So Noelle calls me up this afternoon and says: "Uh, did you talk to Geoffrey?" And I'm like: "Talk to him? The man can't even form complete sentences without the help of his wet nurse, how am I going to talk to him?" And she's like: "Do you think that he likes me?" And I'm like: "Who gives a shit? This is a man who performs somersaults for fun." And she says: "Oh, but he's so intellectual." And I'm like, "Why? Because he refers to his testicles as 'Chang' and 'Eng'? Okay, I'm done.

Robert (laughing): Fabulous!

Martha (laughing): Beautiful.

Mike (laughing): Wow!

Janeane: Seriously, I'm done. Money please.

(Dissolve to a musical montage . . . "I Feel Good," by James Brown)

Cut to:

Janeane, in slow motion, scowling.

Janeane, in slow motion, scowling.

Janeane, in slow motion, scowling.

(Musical montage ends)

Robert: We can't thank you enough.

Janeane: Suck my balls.

(More laughter)

Ext.:

Out of the house Janeane walks, slowly, and with solid
purpose. She is ravishing, in a dark, brooding way. She
is a woman alone against the world, her only weapons
her acerbic wit and her edgy tendencies. She is off to the
Smyths, and to their home movie. They've never had
a sarcastic, progressive maid, and yet they've always
dreamed of employing one. The Sacks family can only
stand back in awe, and wave. The watermelon candle
burns to a slow ember, and then out.

Important Notice:

Dearest Readers:

If you, too, are interested in having Janeane Garofalo
star in your home movie for very little or absolutely
no money, you can reach her through International
Creative Management, 10250 Constellation Blvd, 9th
Floor, Los Angeles, CA 90067. Or, by phone at 310-550-
4000. Please tell her that Mike Sacks, her younger
brother for one joyful, enchanting afternoon, says
"hello."

Dear Family and Estate of John Updike

(A Rhon Penny Letter)

I am a writer named Rhon Penny (silent *h*), and I am no longer married. I am writing to you, the legal custodian(s) of the complete works of John Updike, because I am seeking advice on how to take my (and John's) career to the next level—the financial-wealth level.

Are you a fan of absurd questions? Good. Here's one: Have you read the terrific 1979 novel *Flowers in the Attic*? Of course you have. Not that you even need reminding, but this is the book wherein a brother and sister are locked in an attic, and spend their days playing board games, reading old issues of *National Geographic*, and partaking in incest. It's a lot of fun.

You're thinking: What the heck is Rhon getting at? Well, here's a little secret: the author of this book, V. C. Andrews, died in 1986 . . . and yet, to this day, Miss Andrews still produces obscenely popular books under the V. C. Andrews brand! How in the world does V.C. do it? Guess what . . . she *doesn't*! An alive writer does all of the writing for her! This is where I come into the picture.

Correct me if I'm wrong, but your father, John Updike, was known as "high-falutin'." Meaning, he tended to write books that most people didn't "get" or "buy." And that's fine. Not everyone can be Judy Blume. Truly, you should not feel ashamed. There's little doubt that if I had a menu filled with writers, your father would certainly be one of the main courses. Let's face it, though: he would probably be something like pumpkin octopus risotto, or some other dish that sounds all fancy but no one ever orders.

A little bit about myself: I have more than fifteen years of experience trying to get published, and by extension, much to offer you in your extended period of grief. Until recently, I worked at Kinko's, and I am now on worker's comp (yes, it was "alcohol-related"). I am a fan of body-switching movies and reruns of old game shows, and while I've never been a huge fan of your father's work (too serious and stuck-up), I have a million ideas that just scream out "Put John Updike's name on me!" As you can see from my following ideas list, I'm sort of going through a historical thing right now:

- Has anyone written—I mean really written—about the **Holocaust**? Oh, sure, there have been books and movies and perhaps even a rap song, but has anyone penned a thought-provoking book about the subject? My answer: I'm not sure. Here's my idea: a novel set in Nazi Germany, about an adorable, wisecracking gerbil who lives inside a Jewish person's skull-cap (without that Jewish person's knowledge or consent). The gerbil's name will be Rosco.

- **Slavery** has always bothered me slightly from a moral/ethical/historical perspective. But where to begin? This subject is, let's admit it, a large one. How to tackle it? Where's my "in"? Let me sleep on this one.

- **Bubonic plague** holds a great fascination for me, as I'm sure it does for all of the Updikes. How awful would it have been for a child to be sleeping on his or her straw bed one day, and then the next, to be suffering from an awful bug-transported disease? How would this child have felt? Would it have coughed? Sneezed? Died? All three? This subject is ripe for further investigation. We can also include a scene involving Christmas, if you want the book to be extra, extra popular.

Now, I've been burned in the past by sending out detailed outlines, but for each of the above ideas I can certainly provide you with a hand-drawn illustration of what I am going for—as well as an ironclad promise that most of the action will take place in suburban Pennsylvania, with ample nudity. And that your father and/or husband, John Updike, will have "written it." (Note the quotes.)

Before we talk again, here are some additional ideas that I can't wait to sink my (and your dead father's) teeth into:

- Did your father ever write an episode for a sitcom? How about a screenplay for a movie based on a TV show from the '80s or '90s? No? Let me write this for him.

- Poetry slams were very exciting and hip a number of years back. Let's take advantage of this.

- Children's literature is kind of hot right now. I was thinking that a "John Updike Presents" would be popular, and would be a terrific way to launch our new partnership. Just off the cuff: A boy wants to become a wizard at a magic school, but has to apply for financial aid. I would concentrate on the financial-aid part, and I'd really get into the nitty-gritty of how little wizard boys go about acquiring favorable financial-aid packages and such. And I do mean "as such." But there really does have to be a signed contract before I get into the particulars . . .

- Something to do with "electronic books."

For reasons gastrointestinally based, I must end this correspondence immediately. But I will not leave you without quoting the following (seen on my therapist's paperweight): *Excuses are like butts. Everyone's got 'em, but I don't necessarily want to see 'em.*

Please . . . no excuses. Or buts.

Your partner in literature,
Rhon Penny

Attention Readers!

The Last Word

This is important! Remember that guy I was telling you about earlier in the book? The one who lives across the street from me and who has green orbs for eyes? He's kind of private and withdrawn? The one who can make lightning flash out of his fingers? He died yesterday.

Credits:

Whoops! (*McSweeney's*); A Leaflet Dropped over Amy Weller's House (*The New Yorker*); Saw You on the Q Train (*Esquire*); Outsourcing My Love (*Eyeshot*); IKEA Instructions (*Esquire*); Dear Mister Thomas Pynchon (The Barnes and Noble Review's *Grin & Tonic*); A Short Story Geared to College Students, Written by a Thirtysomething Author (*McSweeney's*); Signs Your College Is Not Very Prestigious (*Radar*); Rules for My Cuddle Party (*McSweeney's*); Geoff Sarkin Is Using Twitter! (*The New Yorker*); Reasons You're Still Single (*Radar*); Opening Lines to the Rough Draft of Rudyard Kipling's "If" (*McSweeney's*); From the Sea Journal of the Esteemed Dr. Ridley L. Honeycomb (The Barnes and Noble Review's *Grin & Tonic*); What in the Hell Is That Thing? FAQ (*McSweeney's*); The Three Laws of Robotics According to Isaac Asimov, Plus Twenty-One According to Me (*Sweet Fancy Moses*); HI, EVERYBODY!!!?? A Paid Advertisement (*The Freedonian*); Some Fabrications to Insert Into a Personal Diary (*McSweeney's*); The Rejection of Anne Frank (The Barnes and Noble Review's *Grin & Tonic*); Dear Mister Don DeLillo (The Barnes and Noble Review's *Grin & Tonic*); Open Mic Night, 1:15 AM (*McSweeney's*); Arse Poetica (*McSweeney's*); The Bachelor Party: What You Need to Know (*McSweeney's*); "Out-of-Office E-Mails" That Might Not Fly with Those in Charge (*McSweeney's*); Jimmy Jam Johnson, the Classic-Rock D.J. Sufferin' a Nervous Breakdown! (*McSweeney's*); Krazy Kris! (*McSweeney's*); FW: Loved the Following Jokes and Thought You'd Love Them As Well! (*McSweeney's*); Things You *Must* Do Before You Grow Too Old (*Radar*); The Zapruder Film: The Novelization (*McSweeney's*); Game-Show Catchphrases That Never Quite Caught On (*McSweeney's*); My Parents, Enid and Sal, Used to Be Famous Porn Stars (*The New Yorker*); Everyday Tantric Positions! (*Vanity Fair*); Hey Babe (*McSweeney's*); When Making Love to Me: What

Every Woman Needs to Know (*McSweeney's*); Icebreakers to Avoid (*Radar*); Dear Mister Salman Rushdie (The Barnes and Noble Review's *Grin & Tonic*); Shaft in the Suburbs (*The Freedonian*); A Few Things I've Discovered about Teenagers (*McSweeney's*); The Ongoing, Insanely Exciting Adventures of the Apple Valley High Gang! (*The Freedonian*); *Kama Sutra*: The Corrections (*Esquire*); Substitute Buddha Master (*McSweeney's*); Worst Places to Die (*Radar*); Funny Letters from Summer Camp and Their Not-So-Funny Responses (*McSweeney's*); Happiness Is . . . (*McSweeney's*); Happiness Isn't . . . (*McSweeney's*); Contract for Your Appearance on *Worst Family in the World*; Director's Commentary (The Barnes and Noble Review's *Grin & Tonic*); Shared Beach House for Rent: Act QUICKLY!; Baseball Boners (Post-Career) (*McSweeney's*); Famous Philosophers and How They Were First Discovered (*McSweeney's*); My Family Home Movie: The 10th Anniversary (*The Freedonian*); Dear Family and Estate of John Updike (The Barnes and Noble Review's *Grin & Tonic*).

A Hearty Thank-You To:

My family

Todd Levin, Scott Jacobson, Bob Powers, Jason Roeder, Scott Rothman, Will Tracy, Ted Travelstead, Teddy Wayne

Susan Morrison

Lizzie Widdicombe

David Sedaris

Merrill Markoe

Dan Bova, Jane Borden, John Branch, Michelle Brower, Rocco Castoro, Punch Hutton, Dave Katz, Adam Laukhuf, Christopher Monks, S. P. Nix, John Warner

Tony Perez

Deborah Jayne, Nanci McCloskey, Janet Parker, and the rest of the amazing staff at Tin House Books

John Banta, Connell Barrett, Mike Batistick, Melanie Berliet, Justin Bishop, Steve Bopp, David Brody, Dana Brown, Mr. and Mrs. Catfish, Leigh Cheng, Natalie Chepul, Jason Cronic, Jason Eaton, Sharon Festinger, Laura Griffin, Sarah Hepburn, Jane Herman, Mike Hogan, Katie I., Todd Jackson, Amelia Kahaney, Kasendorfs, Elyse Kroll, Ian Lendler, Austin Merrill, Whitney Pastorek, the Pengs, Todd Pruzan, Alana Quirk, Dave Reidy, Gina Rhodes, the other Mike Sacks, Julian Sancton, Gabe Sanders, Chris Scott, Sohaila Shakib, Eric Spitznagel, Dana Spivak, Corey and

Cheryl Spound, Strath and Emily, Andy Tepper, Elaine Trigiani, Marie Warsh, Steve Whitesell, Steve Wilson, Jim Windolf, Julie Wright and Claire Zulkey

Gloria and Maria Ayalde

The upstanding citizens of the planned community of New Granada ("Tomorrow's City . . . Today")

Charlie Cocoa, Fritzy the Bumblebee, and The Professor, 143

Bio

Mike Sacks has written for such publications as *The Believer*, *Esquire*, *GQ*, *McSweeney's*, *The New Yorker*, *Premiere*, *Radar*, *Salon*, *Time*, *Time Out New York*, *Vanity Fair*, *Vice*, and *Women's Health*. He has worked at *The Washington Post*, and is currently on the editorial staff of *Vanity Fair*.

His first book, *And Here's the Kicker: Conversations with 21 Humor Writers About Their Craft*, was released in July 2009 by Writer's Digest Books.

His second book, *SEX: Our Bodies, Our Junk*, co-written with Scott Jacobson, Todd Levin, Jason Roeder, and Ted Travelstead, was released by Random House in August 2010.

www.mikesacks.com